# Thinkers' Chess

## A *Compendium of Games,*

including annotations, thoughts, second thoughts, inspiration, and talent gleaned from the Front-Line Field Troops of *Thinkers' Press,* spearheaded and organized (more or less) by noted Field Commander ...

## Stephan Gerzadowicz

Thinkers' Press
Davenport Iowa

1995

THINKERS'
PRESS

First Printing: January 1995
ISBN: 0-938650-65-3

Requests for permissions and republication rights should be addressed in writing to:

> Thinkers' Press
> c/o Bob Long
> P.O. Box 8
> Davenport, Iowa 52805-0008

**Note:** The publisher is interested in a possible sequel to *Thinkers' Chess* and therefore encourages interested customers of Chessco, the chess mail order house (same address as above), to send in one or two of their most interesting games—with or without notes.

No promise is made of publication of either games or the book. If such a book is produced there is no promise that Stephan Gerzadowicz will be the author.

It is not necessary to send games where there was a big difference in ratings—just interesting games—thinkers' chess.

# Dedication

To John Grassilli

*Most Favored Thinker*

# Contents

# Introduction

How best to learn about chess? How best to teach chess? Doubtless there's no best answer.

The general "textbooks" — the Nimzovitch, the Pachman, the Kotov — are all fine, and probably necessary. So, too, are opening, middlegame, and endgame books. They all work — if you do!

But those books are all to a degree contrived, artificial, fragmentary. And that's not a totally Bad Thing.

But I've always more enjoyed books of complete games — "stories" with a Beginning, a Middle, and an End. The drama of the human struggle captures me more than any instructional text can.

But how useful is this? That can depend on the extent and depth of the notes. I went through all the old textbooks, but what I remember most enjoying *and profiting from* were the game collections with long and wordy annotations. Not masses of variations, but words telling you what's going on. The great old Edward Lasker books were particular early favorites. Much of Réti is good in this regard, as is Botvinnik and Bronstein's Zurich '53, and Tal on his first title match, and Cecil Purdy from Down Under. Best of all — for me — was the three-volume *Grandmaster of Chess* series by Paul Keres. He said it — "The notes on the various games should be, I decided, as exhaustively done as possible so as to increase the value of the book as a manual of instruction."

That's what I try to do here.

*Journal of a Chess Master* tended toward that approach; but with a single player's games, his style is a limiting factor. I wanted the widest possible range of games.

But where could we get these games? From Bob Long's CHESSCO customers! They've been buying his books for 25 years; about time they got into one.

When we began soliciting games, I didn't know what to expect. I hoped I wouldn't have to gussy 'em up too much to make them presentable in good company. I needn't have worried. It did not become a case of me making them look good — if anything, I fear it may be the other way around.

We did not have room to use all of the games submitted. I apologize to those whose games we left out. Many of them were the equal of the bulk of what follows, but were left out for "technical," and even arbitrary, reasons — opening duplication and the like. They may appear in a second volume.

The games that follow fell into certain categories, and are grouped accordingly. But they may be played over in any order with equal benefit, and have been indexed by opening, *ECO* code, etc.

Keres again: "With this I hand my work over to the reader. I hope it will find welcome acceptance not only as reading for tournament players but also as a manual for the less advanced player."

Stephen Gerzadowicz
October 1994

# PART I — Development

Coming off a Wimbledon win in the 1960s Rod Laver had a few bad matches. When asked what was wrong with his game he said, "I haven't been watching the ball real well."

Watch the ball.

Develop your pieces.

Everyone knows those two things. But if Laver could forget the first, how much more likely for us to forget the second. And WE have reason! There's so many things to do! Like attack. Or get a Knight to *that* special square. Or tidy up with a bunch of Pawn moves...

Nah.

Get the pieces out.

Watch the ball.

An important game for Black. If he wins, he gets a berth on the US-NATO Team. I don't know if Mr. Rea is still in the service. I suspect he was in the Gulf War. Judging by its result.

## w: Lane Teraoka (2207)
## b: Andy Rea (2137)
Vienna Game C28/2
### US Armed Forces Ch. 9/26/89

| | | |
|---|---|---|
| 1. | e4 | d6 |
| 2. | Nc3 | e5 |
| 3. | Bc4 | Nc6 |
| 4. | d3 | Nf6 |
| 5. | f4 | Be6 |

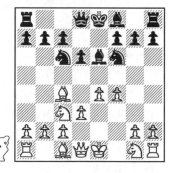

**6.   Bb5?!**

Not a terrible move, but not best. Not necessary. White wastes a tempo, moving the Bishop a second time to avoid doubled pawns on c2 and c4. But doubled pawns are not always bad. How to decide?

Do a cost/benefit analysis. List plusses and minuses, and compare, evaluate. So here after 6. *f5* (say) *Bxc4* 7. *dc4*, what's the downside? Certainly, moving the pawn from d3 to c4 makes White's pawns a *little* weaker, but how bad is it? Black can attack c4 and e4, but they are easily defended, e.g., ...*Na5* is answered by *b2-b3* or, better, *Qd3* with the option of *b2-b4*.

Do the doubled pawns do White any good? Sure. The pawn on c4 helps control the important d5-square. Why important? Look at the Bishop on f8. It is hard for Black to develop it actively. White would like to keep it locked behind those black pawns on dark squares, and the pawn on c4 helps do this. If it suddenly slid from c4 to d3, Black would immediately pop in ...d5!

Any other benefits? More space on the half-open d-file. White can now play *Qd3* and perhaps then *Nd5* and finish a Knight exchange with *Qxd5*. More space, more options.

*And* while the P/c4 covers d5, White can play *c2-c3*, and also take d4 away from Black, and at no great cost. If Black ever plays the corresponding ...c6, his d-pawn becomes weak (open d-file!).

Conclusion? *These* doubled pawns would be *good* for White.

In a like manner, White does not play 6. *Bxe6?* After 6... *fe6* the black pawn would cover more important squares from e6 than it did from f7.

The reason for 6. *f5*, by the way, also has to do with pawns. If instead 6. *Nf3* (say), after 6... *Bxc4* 7. *dc4 ef4* 8. *Bxf4* White's e-pawn is isolated. The problem is not so much that the pawn is weak as that the square in front of it will be so useful to Black— ...*Nd7*, ...*Be7-f6*, ...*Nde5*.

| 6. | ... | ef4 |
| 7. | Bxf4 | a6 |
| 8. | Ba4 | |

Likewise, pawns on c6 and c7 would not be bad for Black.

| 8. | ... | b5 |
| 9. | Bb3 | Bg4 |

*And 9... Bxb3 10. ab3* would only develop White's Rook.

| 10. | Qd2 | Nd4 |
| 11. | h3 | Bh5 |
| 12. | g4 | Bg6 |
| 13. | Qe3 | Nxb3 |
| 14. | ab3 | Nd7 |
| 15. | Nf3 | f6 |

Prepares ...*Bf7* and strengthens e5, but locks the King's Bishop in. *15... Be7* is more flexible; Black can still play ...*f6* later if it then seems good.

| 16. | 0-0 | Qc8 |

Ambitious. White would have a clear advantage after ...*Be7* and ...*0-0*.

| 17. | Rae1 | |

This Rook was well-posted on a1. *17. d4* looks good, as does *17. Rfe1*. Perhaps White did not expect Black to castle Queenside; after that, the Rook obviously belongs on a1.

| 17. | ... | Qb7 |
| 18. | d4 | 0-0-0 |

**19. d5**

It hurts to give Black that great e5-square. White should try to maintain his pawns on d4 and e4 as long as he can. He should play *19. b4* to stop the e4 defender from being driven away by *...b4*. The pawn could always go to d5 later, but now it can never again control e5.

A move like *19. d5 can* be good if it is part of a plan leading to an advantage. That doesn't seem the case here.

| | | |
|---|---|---|
| **19.** | **...** | **Re8** |
| **20.** | **b4** | **Ne5** |
| **21.** | **Nh4** | |

Unfortunately, *21. Nxe5 de5* drops the b-pawn. But the centralizing *21. Nd4* looks better.

| | | |
|---|---|---|
| **21.** | **...** | **Nc4** |
| **22.** | **Qc1** | **Bf7** |
| **23.** | **Bg3** | |

In view of ...g5.

| | | |
|---|---|---|
| **23.** | **...** | **c6?!** |

*23... h5* at once would be better. *...c6?!* risks opening the game when White is ahead in development.

Why does this matter? Development is quantitative—a glance shows who has more pieces out. But there is a qualitative aspect. Some development leads are more meaningful than others. It depends on how open the game is. Why? Development is as development does. With blocked pawns and a few weak points a player can survive a development disadvantage—he will have little mobility, but little need for it. But as the board opens, the number of legal moves increases, and as *that* happens the odds of a move being a cruncher go up.

| | | |
|---|---|---|
| **24.** | **b3** | **Ne5** |
| **25.** | **Qd2** | **h5** |
| **26.** | **dc6** | |

Since it is hard to adequately defend both d5 and g4.

| | | |
|---|---|---|
| **26.** | **...** | **Qb6†** |

To line up Q/c6 versus K/g2. If instead of *27. Kg2* White tries *27. Bf2 Qxc6*, Black would threaten ...g5 and ...Nf3†.

| | | |
|---|---|---|
| **27.** | **Kg2** | **hg4** |
| **28.** | **hg4** | **Qxc6** |
| **29.** | **Nd5** | **Kb7** |

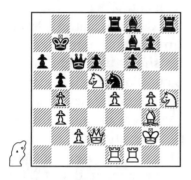

The position is very double-edged. Black is winning the g-pawn, but White has an advantage in development and activity. Thus if immediately 29... Nxg4, Rf3-c3 is dangerous.

So what should White do? He plays 30. Nf5. Centralizing this Knight is a good idea, and might have fit into a winning scheme.

But *overall*, what should White do? With Kings on opposite wings and both rather loosely sheltered, we can expect direct attacks. Nf5-d4 is *good*, but White isn't going to deliver a decisive blow with two Knights. He needs to open lines, to figure out a way to get more pieces heading toward b7. The move 30. c4! suggests itself. The threat is to take on b5 and play Rc1-c7. If Black plays 30... bc4, 31. bc4 is bad because it activates the black Queen after 31... Qxc4 (32. Rc1? Qxe4†). But White can play 30... bc4 31. Rc1! Now White

threatens 32. bc4 and more line-opening with b4-b5. And if the black Knight moves, White could capture on c4 with the Rook. The Big Point is that the pot is boiling where White wants it to—over in front of the black King. This is what Black's 23rd move (...c6?!) should have cost him.

Another reason for 30. c4 is to shore up d5. Look at that long white diagonal. It need not become a factor ... but it sure might. Black has that Bishop on f7 whose white counterpart is gone. You can imagine White's eyes dance—Q or B on e4 or d5, N on g4, white K/g1, Rh8-h1.

I *like* 30. c4.

**30. Nf5        Nxg4**
**31. Rf3**

Last chance for c2-c4!? Or 31. Nd4!? But the move in the game *is* playable.

Now Black plays a rather remarkable Queen sac. See it?

**31. ...        Rxe4!?**

Neither did I. Black is making a virtue of necessity. He can't sit idly and watch Rf3-c3-c7. And he *has* been eyeing that long diagonal.

The point that is easy to miss is that the Rook on e1 helps defend a Knight on e7. Black had to see this, and then see to allow it.

**32. Nfe7        Bxd5**

| 33. | Nxc6 | Bxc6 |
| 34. | Rxe4 | Bxe4 |

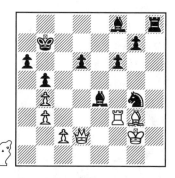

Now White should get his Rook out of the pin by 35. *Qe2!* Suddenly it's awkward for Black! He can't take on f3 because *Qxf3†* will bag the Knight, as would 35... *Bc6 36. Kg1 Bxf3? 37. Qxf3†*. So he must protect the Bishop, but that will drop the protecting pawn after 35... *f5 (...d5) 36. Kg1 Bxf3 37. Qxf3†* and 38. *Qxf5*. Then it's Q versus R+N+P, with Black so undeveloped and cramped that I don't see him avoiding a quick loss.

**35. Bxd6??**

Bad both positionally and tactically. That Bishop on f8 has never even moved, and it is still locked behind its own pawns. Why let it out?

But the tactical flaw is even worse. With the B/g3 gone, Black can attack the helpless Rook a second time.

| 35. | ... | Bxd6 |
| 36. | Qxd6 | Ne5 |

| 37. | Qe7† | Ka8 |
| 38. | Qxg7 | Re8 |

Seeing that it may prove useful to protect the Knight.

| 39. | Qxf6 | Bxf3† |
| 40. | Kg3 | Bb7 |
| 41. | Qd6 | |

If White can trade off all the pawns, he can draw. Even if he doesn't *know* that he should try to trade 'em all off. Why? His are the more vulnerable. How can White ever win a6? But Black can maneuver and maneuver until he attacks a pawn with two pieces. The Queen can't "defend" against that—too much power is gathered in one being. Not very useful in this real world. The Spirit of Democracy permeates the board.

| 41. | ... | Nc6 |
| 42. | Kf2 | |

Can't get the pawns off—42. *c4 Re3† 43. Kf2 Rxb3 44. cb5 ab5* and White can't stop ...*Rxb4*, since 45. *Qf8† Ka7 46. Qc5† Ka6* is no help.

| 42. | ... | Rd8 |
|-----|-----|-----|
| 43. | Qc5 | Nb8 |
| 44. | c4 | Rc8 |
| 45. | Qd4 | Rf8† |
| 46. | Ke1 | Nc6 |
| 47. | Qc5 | Re8† |
| 48. | Kf1? | |

Aloof. Putting the King to work (*48. Kd1*) is a better try. In fact, any square is better than f1. White again has trouble on a white diagonal.

| 48. | ... | Nb8 |
|-----|-----|-----|
| 49. | cb5 | |

Seeing the skewer—*Qb5 Ba6*—White would retain more options by leaving the pawns on. Then he could threaten both a6 and b5. After the text, all Black must defend is b5. And White would not be risking much— Black will hardly consider playing *...bc4*, when the white pawns would be dangerously mobile and the last pawn exchange virtually assured.

He may have been losing anyway; now, he surely is.

| 49. | ... | ab5 |
|-----|-----|-----|
| 50. | Kf2 | Bc6 |
| 51. | Qb6 | |

White is outnumbered. This keeps the Knight and King back, but neglects the pawns. Remember the note to White's 48th.

| 51. | ... | Rf8† |
|-----|-----|-----|
| 52. | Ke1 | Rf3 |
| 53. | Kd2 | Rxb3 |

| 54. | Kc1 | Rc3† |
|-----|-----|-----|

Taking the pawn drops the Rook.

| 55. | Kd2 | Rc4 |
|-----|-----|-----|
| 56. | Ke3 | Nd7 |
| 57. | Qc7 | Re4† |
| 58. | Kd2 | Ne5 |

This is fun. Black keeps finding positions where the pieces protect each other in a ragged circle.

| 59. | Kd1 | Rd4† |
|-----|-----|-----|
| 60. | Ke2 | Rc4 |
| 61. | Qb6 | |

*61. Qxe5? Re4†.*

| 61. | ... | Nf3 |
|-----|-----|-----|
| 62. | Kd1 | Nd4 |
| 63. | Kd2 | Nc2 |
| 64. | Kc1 | Nxb4† |

This was inevitable. Now it's easy—but Black must be careful. The tendency would be to relax. You should fight that by cranking up your intensity a notch.

I once watched a hero of mine, SM John Curdo, playing another Master. Doctor John had Queen and Rook-versus-King, but he was playing very deliberately, looking for maximum efficiency, finding everything there was to think about in the position. A Good Lesson!

| | | |
|---|---|---|
| 65. | Kb1 | Nd5 |
| 66. | Qd8† | Kb7 |
| 67. | Qf8 | Nb6 |
| 68. | Kb2 | Na4† |
| 69. | Ka3 | Nc5 |
| 70. | Kb2 | Nd3† |
| 71. | Ka3 | Rc3† |
| 72. | Ka2 | Bd5† |
| | 0-1 | |

A Lesson for Our Time. Mr. Woodworth—great name for a chessplayer—teaches us that quality can equal quantity.

## w: Robert Woodworth (1950 CC)
## b: John Marconnet (2150 CC)
Grünfeld Defense D93/1
## APCT 89RT-8

| | | |
|---|---|---|
| 1. | d4 | Nf6 |
| 2. | Nf3 | g6 |
| 3. | c4 | Bg7 |
| 4. | Nc3 | d5 |
| 5. | Bf4 | 0-0 |
| 6. | e3 | c5 |

The solid 6... c6 is the main alternative.

The most common reply to the text seems to be 7. dc5, but many moves are possible—7. Qb3, 7. cd5, 7. h3, 7. Be5, and White's choice.

Note that after 7. dc5 Black often plays 7... Qa5 △ 8... Ne4. 7. dc5 opens the diagonal for Black's Bishop and, unlike 7. Be2, does not facilitate castling. Black gets good play, equal chances.

**7. Be2    Qa5**

But here, this move has less point; White castles so fast that the Knight never even feels the pin.

The only example of 7. Be2 I have is Zinn–Uhlmann 1967. Black was a little better after 7... cd4 8. ed4 Nc6 9. 0-0 Bg4 10. c5 Ne4 11. Be3 e6 12. h3 Bxf3 13. Bxf3 f5.

**8. 0-0    Rd8**

Looks good—until you see White's reply.

Black should probably take a pawn. And maybe take 'em both and play ...Bg4 and ...Qh5.

In the game, Black gets into a bit of a bind. How could he have anticipated that? Sheer Tactical Alertness would've done it, of course, but that takes *lots* of energy. Is there a labor-saving device? Well, Black might note that the B/f4 is the most unusually—and actively—placed white piece. Ideally, Black should check *all* of the possibilities of *all* of the pieces. But when it's too much trouble to "round up all the suspects," he should concentrate on the likely ones— e.g., he probably has more to fear from the B/f4 than the R/f1.

**9. Nb5    Na6**
**10. h3**

So Black can't ease the pressure on c7 with ...Nh5.

**10. ...    Bd7**
**11. a4    Bc6**
**12. Ne5    Nd7**
**13. Ng4**

Any exchange would help Black. The fewer pieces there are in total, the fewer there are to be cramped.

**13. ...    Nb6**
**14. b3**

Now Black plays *13... Nb6 (14. b3)* and exchanges pawns on c4. That does not impress— ...Nb6 adds to the congestion.

If I were Black, I'd be getting a little panicky about the Queen situation. There's no *immediate* danger, but you just can't play a whole game with your biggest piece in a box on the edge of the board.

Three things Black might try instead of *13... Nb6*:

*13... Nf6* seeks an exchange

or a repetition—*14. Ne5 Nd7*.

*13... cd4* and *...Rdc8*, to be able to move the Knight on a6.

*13... f6!?* and *...e5*. Playing in the center is a good idea in general, and *...e5* would cut the Bishop off from c7.

**14. ...    dc4**
**15. bc4    f6**
**16. Qb3    g5**

It can't be a good idea to move a pawn in front of the King when so many of the troops are over on the Queenside. Black is in effect behind in development; therefore, he should not be opening the game or making it easier for White to do so.

*16... Nc8!?* △ *...Nd6* looks best.

**17. Bg3    Nc8**

This threatens to win a piece! With the Queen covering c7, the white Bishop is lost after *18... h5 19. Nh2 h4*.

**18. f4**

White solves that problem with a powerful move. The

threat is *19. Be1 Nb4 (19... Qb6? 20. a5) 20. dc5* and Black's Knight is lost. To meet this, Black defends c5 again, but *18... b6* restricts his Queen even more.

| | | |
|---|---|---|
| 18. | ... | b6 |
| 19. | Be1 | Nb4 |
| 20. | Nc7 | h5 |

Black is in big trouble. He would be glad to "sac" the exchange—his Rook on a8 is not much of a factor, while the white Knight is a tiger. And anyway, *20... Rb8?! 21. fg5 fg5 22. Ne6* and *Nxg7* give White a tremendous attack—*d4-d5, Bc3, Nh6*.

But *20... h5* doesn't help matters. After *21. Nh2*, Black's pawns—and Kingside!—would be hard to defend.

But White finds a tactical solution.

| | | |
|---|---|---|
| 21. | fg5 | hg4 |
| 22. | gf6 | Bxf6 |
| 23. | Bxg4 | |

For his piece, White has two pawns and an exposed black King. More than enough, especially considering where all the black pieces are.

| | | |
|---|---|---|
| 23. | ... | Nd6 |
| 24. | Be6† | Kg7 |
| 25. | Rf4 | Be4 |

Before White can play *26. Rg4†* and *27. Qb1*.

| | | |
|---|---|---|
| 26. | Rg4† | Kh8 |

*26... Kf8* would save postage.

| | | |
|---|---|---|
| 27. | Bc3 | Rab8 |

| | |
|---|---|
| **28.** | **Rf1** |

Threatening assorted mayhem. The road to the black King goes through f6, one way or another:

*29. dc5 bc5 30. Bxf6† ef6 31. Rxf6* and *Rh6†*;

*29. Rxf6 ef6 30. dc5 bc5 31. Bxf6† Kh7 32. Rg7† Kh6 33. Qd1.*

White could take the exchange and win, but his move is good, too. *29. Bxg8 Rxg8* would bring Black's Queen-Rook into play! White appreciates that activity can be as valuable as material, that quality can equal quantity. A Lesson for Our Time.

| | | |
|---|---|---|
| 28. | ... | Rg8 |
| 29. | Rff4 | Rxg4 |
| 30. | Bxg4 | cd4 |

Learned. Too late.

White had many good moves. After *31. Nd5* he has a strong attack, whether Black plays BxN or allows NxB. And I bet *31. Rxf6* worked.

| | | |
|---|---|---|
| 31. | ed4 | b5 |

The point, getting the Queen out. If *31... Qg5, 32. Ne6!*—and I bet *31. Rxf6* works.

| | | |
|---|---|---|
| 32. | Nxb5 | Qd8 |
| 33. | Nxd6 | Qxd6 |
| 34. | Rxe4 | Nd5 |
| 35. | Qc2 | Nxc3 |
| 36. | Qxc3 | |

White need only be careful.

| | | |
|---|---|---|
| 36. | ... | Rb1† |

| | | |
|---|---|---|
| 37. | Kf2 | Qh2 |
| 38. | Bf3 | Qg1† |
| 39. | Kg3 | Rc1 |
| 40. | Qd2 | Kg7 |
| 41. | Bh5 | Kh7 |
| 42. | Qd3 | Kh8 |
| 43. | c5 | |

Now and later, the c-pawn's advance is mostly to clear a line for the Queen.

| | | |
|---|---|---|
| 43. | ... | Ra1 |
| 44. | Qb5 | Ra3† |
| 45. | Bf3 | Kh7 |
| 46. | c6 | Qc1 |
| 47. | Qh5† | Kg7 |
| 48. | Rg4† | Kf8 |
| 49. | Qd5 | 1-0 |

Delightful. Mr. Dennis develops his game and doesn't count trifles—until he notes the mates he missed. But what he played seems just as good!

### w: Robert Ives (1640)
### b: Yancy Dennis (1740)
Pirc Defense B09
## 1993 WORLD OPEN, U1800

| 1. | e4 | d6 |
| 2. | d4 | Nf6 |
| 3. | Nc3 | g6 |
| 4. | f4 | |

The Austrian Attack versus the Pirc.

| 4. | ... | Bg7 |
| 5. | h3 | |

Not in the books. What is White's idea? Not a bad one, actually. Certainly, it has the virtue of aggression. He plans *Be3*, *Qd2*, *0-0-0*, and a Kingside attack. *5. h3* is part of that plan — White doesn't want his B/e3 threatened by ...*Ng4*. So is *5. h3* good?

No. Primarily because White has a better way to solve that particular "problem." The most common move here by far is *5. Nf3*. It is good for the usual rea-

sons of development and play toward the center, but here has the added virtue of vacating g1! White can go ahead with *Be3* and *Qd2*, and meet ...*Ng4* with *Bg1*. Then he can look at his options — leave the Bishop there, or play *h3* and reposition it; and he can play *h3* when most convenient for him, least convenient for Black.

Calculating time lost in the possible variations would be very tricky. You would have to factor in how effectively placed the pieces turned out to be.

The Big Point is that at least *Bg1* is reacting to a *move*; *5. h3* is reacting to the possibility of a move.

| 5. | ... | 0-0 |

Fine. But a principled response to *5. h3?!* would be *5... c5!?* After the normal *5. Nf3* John Nunn in *The Complete Pirc* writes, "*5... c5* must be considered Black's most reliable answer to the Austrian Attack. Black immediately breaks up White's pawn centre and heads for a Sicilian-type structure."

If *5... c5* is good versus *5. Nf3*, it certainly is versus *5. h3*. And it serves as yet another example of meeting wing action by play in the center, er, centre.

**6. Be3        c6**
**7. Qd2        a5**

I'd prefer *7... b5*, threatening to chase the defender of e4 away with *...b4*. And it retains the possibility of *...Qa5*, e.g., *7... b5 8. a3 Qa5*, again threatening *...b4*.

Now White could plausibly switch direction — *a4, Be2, Nf3, 0-0*. But note — because of *5. h3?!*, he might then have to deal with *...Nh5-g3*. If he answers *...Nh5* with *Bf2*, there's *...Bh6* and *...e5*. **Life is just simpler without too many pawn moves.**

**8. 0-0-0      Nbd7**
**9. Nf3**

Finally. But too late? Best may be *9. e5*. Remember the idea of undermining e4?

**9. ...        b5**

**10. e5**

Too late — but maybe his best chance. If *10. Bd3*, Black comes fast with *...b4, ...c5, ...Qc7 △ ...c4.*

Now, in the game, what should Black do with his attacked Knight?

**10. ...        b4**

Leave it there, of course. If he moved it and then played *...b4*, White would have *Ne4* with many centralized options.

Now what should White do with his attacked Knight?

**11. ef6**

I don't think so. *He* should *move* it, to b1 (sigh), likely. Black would indeed have a choice of great central Knight squares, but White should at least try to hold his pawn wedge together. Note the resulting pawn structure in the game.

And notice how White seems about a move behind from where he should be here? Know where that move went? Yup — 5.

h3?! The move *alone* isn't that bad; it's the move in combination with such a sharp continuation, where "every move counts." You can afford such as *5. h3* if you can keep things from getting out of hand, e.g., *8. a4!?*

| 11. | ... | bc3 |
| 12. | Qxc3 | Bxf6 |

*12... Nxf6* looks good, too. Either way, with the pawns off e5 Black's pieces are much more effective. He has a sizable advantage here — his King is safe, while ...c5 will open lines to the white King.

**13. Qxc6**

Well, it stops *13... c5*. But with the King on c1, removing a c-pawn is like dropping your drawbridge.

But *13. Qd2* (say) may not be objectively better. After *13... Rb8* or *13... Qc7* (*13... c5? 14. dc5*), Black will play ...c5 and his pieces will flow toward c1 — ...cd4, ...Nc5, ...Be6, doubling on the b- or c-file.

It's hard to say what the best practical chance is. Perhaps it depends on your personality.

| 13. | ... | Rb8 |

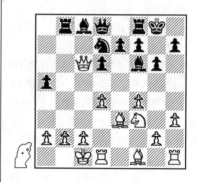

**14. Bb5**

Developing and attempting to get some pieces off. Do you see another way to do this? *All* the black pieces could prove dangerous; but if the white King's Bishop comes off for the Knight, its black counterpart could become a monster on f5 or a6.

I think White should try the unlikely-looking *14. Ba6!?* Then *14... Rb6* is safely met by *15. Qxc8 Qxc8 16. Bxc8 Rxc8*. Black has *great* activity, well worth a pawn, but White may be able to hold. Likewise after *14. Ba6 Bxa6 15. Qxa6 Rb6*. If I were White, I wouldn't feel *good* — but better, for that black Bishop being gone.

| 14. | ... | Rb6 |
| 15. | Qc4 | d5 |

Sensing White's appetite for pawns, he dangles another one before his eyes.

Safest now is surely *16. Qa4 △ Ne5!* I almost prefer White then. But ...

**16. Qxd5**

Munch.

| | | |
|---|---|---|
| 16. | ... | Rd6 |
| 17. | Qb3 | Ba6?! |

Both players disagree with me about the relative values of the black pieces. I think Black should retain this Bishop, and indeed avoid all exchanges with *17... Nb6*, ...*Be6*, ...*Nd5*, ...*Rb6*.

And now in the game White should jump at the chance of *18. Bxa6 Rxa6 19. d5!* He's two pawns up; time to do something for his *pieces* — *Bd4* and *Ne5*, perhaps with *Bxf6* first, *Rhe1*.

| | | |
|---|---|---|
| 18. | Bxd7? | Rxd7 |
| 19. | Ne5 | Rb7 |
| 20. | Qa3 | e6 |

Here again — White is Materially Prosperous; time to do something about the Quality of his Life — *21. d5! ed5 (21... Be7? 22. d6) 22. Bc5 Re8 23. Rhe1* when White is still one pawn up, and all his pieces functioning well. And a5 and d5 are weak. *And* the pawn on d5 denies Black's Queen use of that square.

| | | |
|---|---|---|
| 21. | Nc6? | Qd5 |
| 22. | Nxa5 | |

They're like peanuts, you know.

| | | |
|---|---|---|
| 22. | ... | Be7 |
| 23. | Qc3 | |

*23. Qa4 Rb5* followed by ...*Ra8* and ...*Bb7* doesn't look any better for White.

| | | |
|---|---|---|
| 23. | ... | Bb4 |
| 24. | Qc6 | Qxa2 |

*24... Qxa5* would doubtless win, but Black elects to play for mate.

| | | |
|---|---|---|
| 25. | Nb3 | Ra8 |

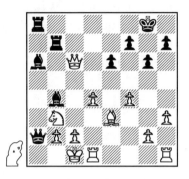

A remarkable array. One threat is *26... Bb5 27. Qxb7 Qa1†*.

| | | |
|---|---|---|
| 26. | c3 | Qxb3 |
| 27. | cb4 | |

Here Mr. Dennis notes that he missed a mate in eight, and gives *27... Bb5 28. Qc3 Rc7 29. Rd3 Ra2 30. Kd2 Rxc3 31. Ke1 Qxb2 32. Bd2 Rxd3 33. Kf1 Qxd2 34. Kg1 Qxg2#*.

Looks right. But his move is not much worse! The important work is to get a position like this. And I find Black's winning method as pleasing as the above.

| | | |
|---|---|---|
| 27. | ... | Qxe3† |
| 28. | Kc2 | Rxb4! |

Calmer approaches also work, e.g., *28... Qe2† 29. Rd2 Qc4†* or *28... Rba7*, ...*Rc8*.

| | | |
|---|---|---|
| 29. | Qxa8† | Kg7 |

30. Qxa6      Qb3†
31. Kd2       Rxd4†
32. Ke2       Re4†
33. Kf1       Qxd1†
34. Kf2

And Mr. Dennis mentions missing a mate here. What he played may be quicker!

34. ...        Qxh1
35. Resigns.

If A, then B. If ...g6, then ...Bg7. Mr. Hecht sets his snare accordingly and C = Black Resigns.

## w: Simon Hecht (1700)
## b: Peter Ash (2008)
Trompowsky Attack A45/11
## CCLA CC 1990

1. **d4**      **Nf6**
2. **Bg5**

The Trompowsky Attack. Octavio Siqueiro F. Trompowsky, one-time Brazilian Champion, played this in the 1930s and '40s. He was born in 1897 and, as far as I know, is still alive. Maybe there's something in 2. Bg5....

2. **...**      **Ne4**
3. **h4**

It sure gets us out of ECO fast. They give only 3. Bh4 and 3. Bf4, so we get to do some original thinking early. It's hard (for me) to say where the Bishop should be. It's easy to say that Black is right to avoid 3... Nxg5 4. hg5 opening the h-file for White. Perhaps he should also avoid the immediate 3... h6. It doesn't seem necessary (except to "prepare" ...e6!), and might be played later as well as — or better than — now.

Indeed, maybe we can more usefully gain time by kicking that Bishop around — one thing 3. h4 does is stop Bh4, so we know that Bf4 is his only active retreat. Maybe we can push him around with ...f6 and ...e5. The f7-square could be weak. Hmmm. Let's get creative here — 3... d5 4. e3 (if f3, ...Nd6) f6 5. Bf4 Be6 △ ...Bf7, ...Nd7, ...e5. If White has played Nf3, ...e6 and ...Bd6 △ ...e5.

Is this great? No. Good? Barely. Playable? Sure. I bet it's as sound as a lot of Black openings. And we've done some original thinking and doubtless dodged any White preparation! Mr. Hecht noted that 3. *h4* is "an idea from Hodgson."

| 3. | ... | h6 |
| 4. | Bf4 | d5 |
| 5. | e3 | Nc6 |

In double d-pawn endings, it's generally not a good idea to play ...*Nc6* before ...*c5*. *Bb5* and *Nf3-e5* can come fast, especially powerfully after ...*Bf5* and ...*e6*. And with the pawn on c7, Black doesn't have the defense ...*Rc8*.

Better 5... *Nd7* 6. *Nd2 Ndf6.* And that avoids ...*Ngf6-e4xd2*; after 7. *Qxd2* the energy of those three Knight moves has disappeared.

| 6. | Nd2 | Nxd2 |
| 7. | Qxd2 | Bf5 |
| 8. | Nf3 | a6 |

Not liking 8... *e6* 9. *Bb5*, though 9... *Bd6* would deal with the worst of it.

| 9. | Bd3 | Bxd3 |
| 10. | Qxd3 | e6 |
| 11. | Ne5 | |

| 11. | ... | Ne7? |

Congesting. I'd (almost always) prefer development, and would willingly suffer the doubled pawns after 9... *Bd6* 10. *Nxc6 bc6±*.

**12. g4**

With his lead in development, White can try to advance, open things up.

| 12. | ... | c5 |

Black, on the other hand, should first get his pieces untangled. The cumbersome ...*Nc8-d6* looks better.

| 13. | c3 | c4? |

Reducing his own options, accomplishing little. 13... *Rc8!?* △ ...*Nc6*, ...*Be7*, or ...*Bd6* is indicated.

| 14. | Qc2 | Nc8 |
| 15. | Ke2 | |

This shows a problem with 13... *c4?* — the white King is safer here than it should be. White plans *Rag1*.

| 15. | ... | h5? |

Get the *pieces* out. 15... *Nd6!?*, 16... *Be7*.

**16. g5**

Now Black understandably fears 17. *g6! f6* 18. *Nf7*, but his solution — a pawn move — is not best. ***It is almost always best to try to solve your problems by activating your pieces; that activity might well prove useful for more than defense.*** And pawn moves usually tend to be committing — they can't go home again. After *16... g6?*, the possibility of *Nxg6* hangs in the air.

**16. ... g6?!**
**17. Raf1**

Does no harm; not particularly useful. With White's development advantage (look at the black pieces!), he could profitably work to open the game with *17. b3* or *17. e4!?*, or *17. f3* and *e4*.

The Alert Reader will not be surprised to learn that I now suggest ... *17... Nd6!*

**17. ... Bg7?**
**18. Nxg6! fg6**
**19. Qxg6† Kf8**

The trouble with *17... Bg7?* is that the King can't now run to the Queenside. So White gets a third pawn.

**20. Qxe6**

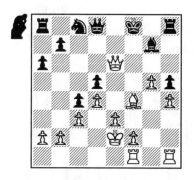

Can Black hold? He can't move much! *20... Nb6 21. Bd6†* identifies one pitfall. He can't move his King or Bishop, ...*Rg8* does not impress, even less does

*20... Rh7? 21. g6.* Queen moves lose d5. *20... Ne7 21. Bd6 △ Rh3-f3* is grim. One good try is *20... a5 △ ...Ra6*; but *21. g6 Qf6 22. Qxd5 Qxg6 23. Rhg1 (△ Rg5-f5) Qd3 (c2)† 24. Kf3* looks winning for White, whose King is considerably safer than Black's.

Black tries for active counterplay, but it's too late, with too little development. And, in general, trading b2 for d5 is a good deal for White.

**20. ... Qb6**
**21. Qf5†**

Okay, but I like *21. Qxd5*. The King is actually safer on e8. On f8, there's danger in both *g6-g7* and perhaps *Qd8†*.

**21. ... Ke8**
**22. Qxd5 Qxb2†**
**23. Kf3 1-0**

Defending a lost position can be fun if you can create complications with active pieces, but there's little joy for Black here. Probably, he should cover c4 with *23... Qb5 (23... Qxc3 24. Qxb7) 24. Qe6† Kd8*, but White would surely win with *25. Rb1 (25. Qf7!?) Qc6† 26. Qxc6 bc6 27. Rb4* or *27. Rb7*. And sooner or later White will move his King and Bishop and play *e4, f5, e5, f5, ... etc.!*

**THE FRYING PAN**: Remarkable. I was gearing up to explain a positional squeeze when Mr. Hilbert saw that his development advantage was just enough . . . to sac a Rook. So I sat back and enjoyed the show.

**w: John Hilbert (1268)**
**b: Peter Lukacs (1376)**

King's Indian Defense E69/10
## USCF GOLDEN KNIGHTS, 1980

| | | |
|---|---|---|
| 1. | d4 | Nf6 |
| 2. | c4 | g6 |
| 3. | g3 | |

Entering a variation more common in the 1940s and '50s, especially at the highest level. Most of the noted Kasparov King's Indian games have started 3. Nc3 Bg7 4. e4. But that does not mean White's fianchetto system is any less good. And it may be a small surprise for Black, and so be a good practical choice.

ECO's move order for this variation is 3. Nc3 Bg7 4. Nf3 d6 5. g3. Either way is fine. But White should note one point — versus either 3. Nc3 or 3. g3, Black can play 3... d5. If White has a fondness for Grünfeld systems with 3. Nc3, he should obviously favor the ECO move order, Hilbert's if he likes 3. g3 d5.

Of course being basically cantankerous I, like Mr. Lukacs, play 4... 0–0 ...

| | | |
|---|---|---|
| 3. | ... | Bg7 |
| 4. | Bg2 | 0–0 |
| 5. | Nf3 | d6 |
| 6. | 0–0 | Nbd7 |
| 7. | Nc3 | e5 |
| 8. | e4 | |

While objectively no better than other variations, this could prove frustrating to a Black player used to countering an early *d4-d5* with a quick ...*f5*, with the players vigorously attacking on opposite wings. Here, White is less committing. He delays *d4-d5*, often sets up with *h3*, *Be3*, *Qc2*, Rooks to the center, and plays *d5* or *de5* or neither, as he *then* thinks best. If Black plays ...*ed4* White has a slight space advantage and persistent pressure on the open d-file.

Not that Black can't survive this! With such as ...*c6*, ...*Qb6* or ...*Qa5*, ...*Re8*, maybe ...*ed4* with ...*Nc5* or ...*Ne5* and ...*Be6*, he can find good squares for most of his pieces — and in a postal game have time to get used to his position. In an OTB game, a prepared White player could have a big familiarity edge in the coming maneuvering.

Now Black has tried many moves, especially 8... *ed4*, 8... *Re8*, and 8... *a6*, but our game's 8... *c6* is most common. Black judges that getting the Queen out and controlling d5 are worth the weakening of d6.

**8. ...        c6**
**9. h3**

On e3, White's Bishop will watch both wings. But an immediate 9. *Be3* is met by 9... *Ng4*, when 10. *Bg5 Qb6* is said to lead to equality. Thus 9. *h3* to stop

...*Ng4*.

Now 9... *Re8* is a little more usual than 9... *Qa5* or Black's move in our game.

**9. ...        Qb6**

With a threat. See it? He attacks d4 again. So what? It's attacked twice, defended twice, right? Ah, but there's a third attacker lurking on g7. And after 10... *ed4* 11. *Nxd4 Nxe4* its presence is seen; Black wins a pawn.

White commonly deals with this by 10. *Re1* so that 12. *Rxe4* covers d4 again. Or he moves the target pawn by 10. *d5* or 10. *de5*. 10. *Re1* is probably best, sitting on his space advantage.

Instead, White plunges us into complications.

**10. c5**

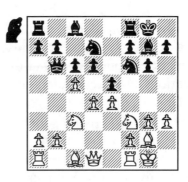

At first glance, you wonder why White puts a pawn on a square attacked three times. Then you see that White is hitting the base of Black's (very small) pawn chain, and will answer 10... *dc5* with 11. *de5*. That

this is not White's best try can only be decided by a tactical analysis, but general considerations also suggest that evaluation. White's "loose" pawn on e5 looks more vulnerable than Black's on c5, the black fianchettoed Bishop has more potential targets than the white, and Black is already attacking white pawns (b2 and e5).

Received Wisdom bears this out — the main line is judged unclear after *10... dc5 11. de5 Ne8 12. Na4 Qa6 (...Qc7=) 13. Bg5 b5 14. Nc3 Nc7 15. Be7 Re8 16. Bd6 Ne6.* Other variations do not substantively change this evaluation, but they immediately become beside our point because Black plays a questionable move.

**10. ...        Qb4?!**

Why? It could be a "normal" mistake, an oversight, or a miscalculation. I offer two other explanations, if only to alert The Reader of things to avoid.

— "*10... dc5* is the obvious move. White wants me to play that, therefore I'd better not." *Wrong.* Give the opponent credit for being able to find good moves — and to find mistakes. Play the position.

— Or, he analyzed *10... dc5* at length, saw some real or imagined dangers, said, "I can't do *that*," and jumped to *10... Qb4*

with much less analysis. The old Frying-Pan-To-Fire Variation, whereas equal time on both moves would likely show *...Qb4* the Greater Evil.

**11. cd6**

Perhaps Black now planned *11... Qxd6 12. de5 Nxe5??*, missing that his Queen hangs. (After *12... Qxd1 13. Rxd1 Ne8* White has *14. Bf4* or the *Bg5-e7-d6* idea.)

Did he then turn too quickly to *11... Re8?!* I don't want to speculate overmuch on subjective reasons for Black's moves, but he does seem to reject obvious moves. Not to say obvious moves are necessarily best. But some players have a tendency to avoid the obvious move *because* it's an obvious move. These labels don't help. Just look at the moves and give the "obvious" *at least* equal time!

Thus, here I'd look at *11... ed4.* If it seems insufficient, look elsewhere, *11... Re8*, say. But don't give up entirely on *11... ed4*. Make sure *11... Re8* is at least as good. Here, I don't think it is.

On *11... ed4* White can recapture with the Queen or Knight. *12. Qxd4 Qxd4 13. Nxd4* allows the old *13... Nxe4* trick. After *14. Nxe4 Bxd4 15. Rd1* I'm not sure if d6 is strong or weak. I'd say unclear, but that's a cop-out. How about "A position with chances for both sides that may well be in dynamic equilibrium"? What does that mean? Means unclear.

But I think we can leave it there, because the other recapture looks a little better. On *11... ed4 12. Nxd4 Qxd6 (12... Nxe4? 13. Nxc6!* is tricky, but I think *13... Nxd6 14. Ne7† Kh8 15. a3* comes out better for White), *13. Nf5!?* and White gets one of Black's Bishops for his Knight *(13... Qxd1 14. Ne7† or 13... Qc5 14. Nxg7)*, and on this open board that would give a lingering, if small, advantage.

But still, that seems a Frying Pan. Instead ... well, let's coin a term. Black is a Pantifier.

| 11. | ... | Re8? |
| 12. | Nxe5 | Nxe5 |
| 13. | de5 | Rxe5 |
| 14. | f4 | Re6 |
| 15. | e5 | Nd7 |

All pretty reasonable, if not forced. Now White's *16. Qe2* covers b2 so he can kick Black's Queen and answer a check with Be3. Black clearly can't live with those white pawns in his face. He will play ...f6 and may even trade that pawn for two of White's. The trouble is that while he's repairing his self-induced damage, he will not be completing his development, and his disadvantage will be translated to one in that sphere.

| 16. | Qe2! | f6 |
| 17. | a3 | Qb3 |

Another point of *16. Qe2* is that if *17... Qa5* (say) *18. b4 Qd8*, White can pin the Rook with *19. Qc4*. Black can deal with this — *19... Nb6 20. Qb3 fe5* — but he's struggling to get his feet out of the flames while White has the happy choice of proceeding calmly *(21. Rd1)* or actively *(21. f5!?)*.

Note the Good Thinking by White — ...f6 is inevitable; that weakens the light-square diagonal that Black's King and Rook are on; how do I get to that diagonal?

Black also sees the diagonal, but b3 is not a safe observation post.

Thus White might now push his a-pawn a little farther. *18. a4!? fe5 19. Ra3 Qb6† 20. Be3 Qd8 21. Ne4* gives him a mighty lead in development, with such as *Qc4* and *Ng5* in the air....

But White finds a — perhaps — even better move. Bolder, certainly.

**18. Rf3        fe5**
**19. Ne4        Qa4**

Now I think *20. f5* is good for White, leaving the pawn on e5 to block the activity of Black's own pieces. After *20... gf5 21. Rxf5*, Black has serious development problems, since a Knight move allows *Nc5*.

Instead, White finds a remarkable move.

**20. b4!?**
Exposing his Rook. Why? Remember that key diagonal?

**20. ...        ef4**
**21. Bxf4        Bxa1**
**22. Qa2        Bd4†**
**23. Kh2        Nf8**
So. Is *this* worth a Rook?
**24. Be3!**

Fighting for c5, among other things. If the Bishop retreats (*...Bg7*), White has *25. Nc5* followed by *Rxf8* and *Nxe6*. Then he'll only be down an exchange, with a dangerous passed pawn and (still!) a development advantage.

So Black takes, doubtless happy to "simplify," expecting *25. Rxe3 Qd1 △ 26. Nc5 Qxd6—+.*

But White's point is to divert the Bishop from *either* c5 or f6.

**24. ...        Bxe3**
**25. Nf6†        Kf7**

If *25... Kg7*, he can't run to e8, so after *26. Qa1* or *Qb2* it looks even better for White than the game.

After White's *26. Qa1* Black can't safely move his King — or much else in the vicinity. His extra Rook and Bishop are only important if he survives....

**26. Qa1        Qb3**
**27. Nh5†        Ke8**
**28. Rxf8†**

Bravo — but what if he takes the Rook?! Instead, he ... *resigns!*

Remember the black Bishop trying to cover c5 and f6? After *28... Kxf8 29. Qg7† Ke8* his Rook "must" cover e7 and f6. Can't do it. *30. Nf6†* and mate next move. Bravo indeed!

White walks a fine and dangerous line while The Reader is subjected to a dose of Zen Thoreauvianism.

### w: Anthony Tempske (2215)
### b: Robert Kostanski (2058)
Ponziani Opening C44/11
## USCF 92 CM 27

| 1. | e4 | e5 |
|---|---|---|
| 2. | Nf3 | Nc6 |
| 3. | c3 | |

Lorenzo Domenico Ponziani (1719-96) was a priest and lawyer. ∞.

| 3. | ... | Nf6 |

This and 3... *d5* are the main moves here. Ponziani's only contribution to this opening, named for him, was to suggest the inferior 3... *f5*.

| 4. | d4 | Nxe4 |
|---|---|---|
| 5. | d5 | Nb8 |

There is a more complicated move and a less complicated move.

5... *Bc5 6. dc6 Bxf2†* is not for the faint of heart. Sax in *ECO* calls it unclear after 7. *Ke2 bc6 8. Qa4 f5 9. Nbd2 0-0 10. Nxe4 fe4 11. Qxe4 Bb6 12. Kd1! d5 13.*

*Qxe5 Bf5!*

5... *Ne7 6. Nxe5 Ng6* tends to lead to exchanges and equality.

5... *Nb8* tries for more than merely swopping off White's N/e5. Does the black Knight "waste time"? To a degree, but the White moves that caused it (*3. c3, 5. d5*) are not all that dangerous to Black. ...*Nc6-b8* would be a sign of trouble if White had been getting a piece out on every turn.

| 6. | Nxe5 | |

Now 6... *Bc5* is again complicated, but it's not a piece sac after 7. *Qg4 0–0* 8. *Qxe4 d6* because of the idea ...*Re8*. It's again unclear after 9. *Bd3 f5* 10. *Qc4 b5* 11. *Qxb5 Qe7*.

**6. ...        Bd6**

And now White has three moves.

That ...*Re8* idea showed up in Alburt–Zuhovickij 1968—7. *Qd4 0–0* 8. *Qxe4 Bxe5=*.

And 7. *Nd3* was equal after 7... *0–0* 8. *Be3 Re8* 9. *Be2 Bf8* 10. *Nd2 Nxd2* 11. *Qxd2 d6*, Makropoulos–Matanovic 1981.

White's move may be new. And equal.

|       |        |        |
|-------|--------|--------|
| 7.    | Nc4    | Bc5    |
| 8.    | Be3    | 0–0    |
| 9.    | Bd3    | Bxe3   |
| 10.   | Nxe3   | Nf6    |
| 11.   | 0–0    |        |

White has a tiny lead in development. The pawn on d5 confers a bit of a space advantage, but it's a mixed blessing. The advance has left good black-Knight posts behind on c5 and e5, and the fixed pawns on d5 and d6 make Black's Bishop a little more valuable than White's. But this is a long-term consideration. A Bishop is hardly "bad" when it has as much scope as White's does here. But in a simple ending, the Bishop could be reduced to defense.

|       |        |        |
|-------|--------|--------|
| 11.   | ...    | d6     |
| 12.   | Nd2    | Nbd7   |
| 13.   | Re1    | Ne5    |
| 14.   | Be2    |        |

14. *Bc2* appears more active, continuing to target h7, but White wants to avoid exchanges on g4. His space and his Bishop both argue for keeping pieces on the board.

|       |        |        |
|-------|--------|--------|
| 14.   | ...    | Re8    |
| 15.   | Qb3    | c6     |

Playable perhaps, but questionable. White still has a small lead in development; Black should hesitate to open lines. If it's a good idea at all, ...c6 could be played later.

A small point, but these quiet positions can be dangerous. One or two indifferent or inattentive moves, and a position can slip away....

*"Attention must be paid."*
—Linda Loman

Life is like Chess. Every instant is more interesting, more valuable, if you give it your full attention. If you find yourself "just making moves," it's time to put the pieces—at least!—back in the box.

> "... I wished to live deliberately, to front only the essential facts of life, and see if I could not learn what it had to teach, and not, when I came to die, discover that I had not lived. I did not wish to live what was not life, living is so dear; nor did I wish to practice resignation ..."
>
> —Thoreau

Am I loading too much baggage onto a move that isn't all *that* bad? I don't think so. I've played and analyzed with students who sit on the edge of their seats when they have a sharp, tactical position—which they handle well. Then they collect their losses in positions just like this one.

More from Thoreau —

> "In any weather, at any hour of the day or night, I have been anxious to improve the nick of time, and notch it on my stick too; to stand on the meeting of two eternities, the past and future, which is precisely the present moment; to toe that line."

I think Black should play ...Ne5-d7-c5, ...a7-a5, ...Bd7, maybe then ...c6, all subject to White's activity.

**16.    c4                 b6?!**

Even more questionable. I still like *16... Ne5-d7*, etc. Perhaps Black expected to have a white pawn on d5 to attack, missing a tactical point in the game continuation. If so, he could have begun with *16... cd5*.

If White had nothing better, he could now simply play *17. dc6* with a pawn-structure advantage. Black would get good piece activity, but not enough to compensate for the weakness of d6.

**17.   f4**

White kicks the Knight away from the defense of c6. But that's not his final point. He must see that Black can't pick up the white pawn that appears on that square.

| 17. | ... | Ng6 |
|---|---|---|
| 18. | dc6 | Nxf4 |
| 19. | Bf3 | Rb8 |
| 20. | Nd5 | |

The Point. Black must take the Knight, allowing White to solidify the pawn on c6. Black's only other try to control c7, *20... Ne6*, fails to *21. Rxe6 Bxe6 22. c7*.

I'm tempted to trot Henry out again ...

| 20. | ... | N6xd5 |
|---|---|---|
| 21. | cd5 | Bf5 |
| 22. | Rxe8 | |

Now *White* relaxes into imprecision. He apparently calculated that this takes the black Queen away from d6, then he attacks d6, then Black "must" defend d6 ..., missing a tactical

point. But tactics aside, White should be leery of giving up the only open file. Better *22. Nc4* at once, or *22. Ne4!?*

Henry? Yeah, why not? —

*Every man is tasked to make his life, even in its details, worthy of the contemplation of his most elevated and critical hour."*

| 22. | ... | Qxe8 |
|---|---|---|
| 23. | Nc4 | |

Perhaps expecting *23... Qe7 24. Qe3*, when White is in great shape. But Black has an important *zwischenzug*.

| 23. | ... | Bd3 |
|---|---|---|

Cutting off e3 so that if *24. Nxd6, ...Qe3†* is possible, after which *25. Kh1 Nh3! (△ 26... Qg1† 27. Rxg1 Nf2#) 26. gh3 Qxf3†* gives Black a perpetual—at least.

I still think White is winning, and if he *knew* that—all praise. But I would have liked to avoid the Black activity.

| 24. | Kh1 | Qe7 |
| 25. | Qb4 | |

Again attacking d6, which Black again meets tactically, at least for one move.

| 25. | ... | Re8 |
| 26. | Rg1 | Bxc4 |

And certainly not the passive *26... Rd8? 27. Re1*.

| 27. | Qxc4 | Qe3 |

The threat is *28... Nh3 29. gh3 Qf3† 30. Rg2 Re1†*.

| 28. | Qc3 | |

If *28. Qf1* (ugh), Black should have enough activity to draw, e.g., *28... Nd3 29. g3 Ne5 30. Bg2 Nd3 31. Bf3....*

The move played gives Black the (barely inadequate) try of *28... Qxc3 29. bc3 Kf8*, when White can't break in if Black manages *...Ne5, ...Kc7*, and *...a5*. White would have to hurry with *Rb1* and *a4-a5*—but not too fast! *30. Rb1 Re3!* threatens to get the Rook behind the pawn, giving Black time to wobble the King over. If then *31. c4 (31. Rb3? Re1#; 31. Rc1 Nd3 32. Rb1 Ne5) Ke8* Black can hold.

White would have to find the precise *30. g3*, when Black's best-looking move, *30... Nd3*, interferes with the *...Re3* idea, thus *31. Rb1 Re3* when not *32.*

*Bg4? Nf2†* or *32. Bg2 Ke8*, but *32. c7! Re8 33. Be2! (△ Ba6, so ...) Nc5 34. Bg4.*

So instead of *31... Re3* (after *30. g3 Nd3 31. Rb1*) Black must try to get the King over. *31... Ke7* works against the hasty *32. a4?! Kd8 33. Kg2 (33. a5 Re1†!) Re1!* But White has *32. Be2*, when wherever the Knight goes White can make the *a4-a5* idea work.

Still, I think this was Black's best practical chance. And that White should have avoided it on Move 22.

| 28. | ... | Nd3 |
| 29. | h3 | Nf2† |
| 30. | Kh2 | Qf4† |
| 31. | g3 | Qg5 |
| 32. | Bg2? | |

Aargh. "Henry nods!" *32. c7* wins. When Black stops the pawn his Knight is trapped on f2. But after *32. Bg2?* Black has *32... Re3 33. Qxe3 Qxe3 34. c7 Qc5 35. Re1 Kf8-+.*

Thus we get a final lesson on Alertness—from both players. There are no routine positions.

| 32. | ... | Qh5? |
| 33. | Rf1 | Resigns |

If *33... Ng4† (best?) 34. Kg1 Ne5*, the double attack *35. Qa3* is convincing.

## PART II — On Exchanging

*My true love hath my heart and I have his,*
*By just exchange one for the other giv'n;*
*I hold his dear, and mine he cannot miss,*
*There never was a better bargain driv'n.*
                                        —*Sir Philip Sidney*

Alas, it's not always so clear. Some players tend to make exchanges, some to avoid them. Both are wrong. Exchanges are just moves. They make changes—good, bad, or indifferent—and those are what must be judged.

Tom Brochard knows more than Tom Hartmayer about Tom Jefferson.

**w: Tom Brochard (1839)**
**b: Tom Hartmayer (1994)**

Colle System D00/14

## 1993 SOUTHERN NEW ENGLAND OPEN

1. d4      Nf6
2. e3      e6
3. Bd3     c5
4. c3

*4. c4* or *4. Nf3* seems more ambitious; but The Colle System, signaled by *4. c3*, can pack a wallop. Versus normal Black development, say *...d5*, *...Be7*, *...0-0*, *...Nc6*, White will play *Nf3, 0-0, Nbd2, Re1*, and look to come out of his crouch with *e3-e4*. It's pretty innocuous, but Black must remain alert. White also has the option of adopting a Stonewall setup with *f2-f4*.

Now Black should play one of the moves mentioned above. Instead, he plays *4...cd4?!*

The Folly of Acquisitiveness! *Taking* something seems so natural; it increases your Store of Treasure. How can it be bad? I have the feeling the very possibility of an exchange looms up before a player's eyes so that other more humdrum moves are barely visible. So he makes the swop — "There, that takes are of *that.*" — as an inevitability, and then looks to get on with his life.

Wrong.

*All moves are created equal.*
— Thomas Jefferson

Not equal in merit, but politically equal, deserving of the same chance to be considered, to run for office, as everyone else. No special consideration just because you happen to be a Capture or have two Zs in your name, reasonable as that may seem.

All moves have consequences. Examine them. Then decide, evaluate. In the game, Black "exchanges on d4." But that's a poor description of what actually happens — what happens is that the pawns on c5 and e3 disappear. Are those pawns equal in quality, in influence? Hardly. The P/c5 is on Black's 4th rank, attacking a center square; the P/e3, on the 3rd, is merely defending. And it blocks in White's Queen's Bishop. Look at the position after the exchange. White's pawn influence in the center is virtually unchanged. Black's is gone.

Why should Black at least defer ...c5xd4? Because the possibility restricts White. After ...d5, White must consider the vulnerability of d4 if he looks at playing c4 or e4.

If he retains his c-pawn, need Black fear d4xc5? Hardly. That would cause the pawns on c5 and d4 to disappear. Trading c5 for d4 is much better for Black than c5 for e3. Look at the position with c5 and d4 gone. White's influence in the center is much reduced, and 2. e3 and 4. c3 have lost much of their point.

That's how to start thinking about this position; that's good, sturdy advice, but it's not absolute. ...c5xd4 *could* be part of a reasonable plan (see next note), as could d4xc5 (e.g., as in a Slav reversed — a3, b4, c4). But both of these ideas suggest some specific opening preparation; you don't need to know nuthin' to play 4... d5.

In our game, after 4... cd4, 5. cd4 is playable but tame. Better to free the Queen's Bishop and go for an open file to call your own.

| 4. | ... | cd4?! |
| --- | --- | --- |
| 5. | ed4 | Nc6 |
| 6. | Nf3 | Be7 |
| 7. | 0-0 | b6 |

It looks better to "minority attack" White's pawn chain with ...d5, ...Rb8 (or ...a6), ...b5-b4. Black would be a move behind a position usually played by White, but at least he would have a plan.

Another idea, solid but passive, would be to deny White e5 with ...d6, develop with ...Bd7 and ...Qc7, and delay committing the King as long as possible, maybe even challenging the White center with ...e5.

| 8. | Bf4 | Bb7 |
| --- | --- | --- |
| 9. | Nbd2 | d5 |

Again, ...d6 comes into consideration. White is focusing a lot of attention on e5; why hand it over so willingly?

| 10. | Re1 | Qc8 |
| --- | --- | --- |

Black's game is difficult. He has made individually reasonable-looking moves, but they do not fit together well. He has not thought enough about what he will *do*. He should have done something to get White's attention (*...b5-b4*), developed a bit more rapidly, or hindered White's free-flowing student-body right idea (*...d6*).

**11. Ne5**

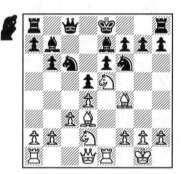

**11. ...          0-0?**

Now I think he's lost. He has delayed castling so far; he should continue to do so, probably with *11... Nxe5* to get some wood off and be able to continue with his plan of *...Ba6*.

What's wrong with *11... 0-0?* The vulnerability of h7. White can attack it a second time with *Qf3-h3*, then work to remove the defending Knight. Black will have to respond with a Weakening Pawn Move....

|       |       |       |
|-------|-------|-------|
| 12.   | Qf3   | Na5   |
| 13.   | Qh3   | Ba6   |
| 14.   | Bc2   | Nc4   |
| 15.   | Ndxc4 | Bxc4  |

**16. Bg5**

Now *16... g6* would weaken f6, and that square is easier to attack than to defend — *17. Qh4 Kg7* (*17... Qd8 18. Nc6*) *18. Bh6†* or *18. Re3* (△ *-f3*).

|       |       |       |
|-------|-------|-------|
| 16.   | ...   | h6    |
| 17.   | Bxh6! | gh6   |
| 18.   | Qxh6  |       |

Rook up-and-over is the threat.

|       |       |       |
|-------|-------|-------|
| 18.   | ...   | Ne4   |
| 19.   | Bxe4  | de4   |
| 20.   | Rxe4  |       |

*20. Re3!* is quicker, but I will forgive White *this* capture.

|       |       |        |
|-------|-------|--------|
| 20.   | ...   | f5     |
| 21.   | Re3   | Bh4    |
| 22.   | Qxh4  | Resigns |

Mr. Tykodi generously shares a learning experience with us. May we all profit.

**w: Ralph Tykodi (1740)**
**b: Charles Gelinas (2010)**
Budapest Defense A52/13
## SE MA CC Rated Game Nov. 1992

| 1. | d4 | Nf6 |
| 2. | c4 | e5 |

The Budapest Defense. Playable, certainly; a bit theoretically suspect—it should not be so easy to challenge White's center! Getting this move in costs Black some time with his Knight. He does get actively placed pieces; but White's development is no worse, and he usually maintains the slight space advantage of a pawn on the 4th versus one on the 3rd—c4 versus d6.

How should you play White if you are not (or are!) familiar with this opening? With straightforward, sensible development.

| 3. | de5 | Ng4 |
| 4. | Nf3 | Nc6 |
| 5. | Nc3 | Bc5 |
| 6. | e3 | Ngxe5 |

| 7. | Nxe5 | Nxe5 |
| 8. | Be2 | 0-0 |
| 9. | 0-0 | Re8 |
| 10. | a3 | |

When is a pawn move a waste of time?

With the pawn on e3, it makes sense to develop the Queen's Bishop on b2. So White could reasonably play *10. b3,* "spending" one move on a good cause. *10. a3* seems slower, but threatens *11. b4 Be7* (or *...Bf8*), when White's two moves have caused Black to use one which has not helped his position. So *10. a3, 11. b4* would only cost White one "move unit."

| 10. | ... | a5 |

Likewise—*10. a3 a5* is a wash. So now *11. b3* doesn't cost any more than *10. b3,* and White judges that his position is a little better—at least no worse—for having the a-pawns up.

| 11. | b3 | d6 |
| 12. | Bb2 | Re6 |

Artificial-looking. Surely, White hasn't played so badly that Black can justify an attack when a little behind in development.

ECO criticizes *12... Qh4* as also premature, giving "13. Nd5 △ b4±; 13. Nb5±."

Their obvious suggestion is to get the Bishop out: *12... Bf5 13. Nb5 c6 14. Nd4 Bd7 15. Qd2 △ b4* is judged only slightly better for White.

| 13. | Nd5 | Qh4 |

*"Black continues his attack. If he tries to dislodge the central Knight by 13... c6, there follows 14. Nf4 Re8 (not 14... Rf6 or 14... Rh6 because of 15. Bxe5!) and his attack has to be put on hold for a while.*

*White could now win a pawn by 14. Nxc7, but at the cost of decentral-izing his Knight and strengthening Black's attack: 14... Rh6, etc."*

—Tykodi

Indeed, I think *14... Rh6* would win in that position—and in the one in the game! That threat is so strong that I think this is a rare case where a King-shielding pawn move is justified. After *14. g3 Rg6 (14... Qh3 15. Nf4) 15. Nf4 Rg5*, White is on the attack: *16. Bxe5 de5 17. Qd8† Bf8 18. Kh1 (18. Nd5? Rxg3† and ...Qxd8) Qh6 19. Nd5*, and I don't see a good defense to *20. Ne7†*, as a Queen move hangs the Rook, a pawn move allows *20. Ne7†, 21. Nxc8*.

Given that, Black must reply to *14. g3* with *14... Qd8*, when *now 15. b4* is great for White.

**14. b4**

A fascinating moment. It's no secret to anyone in the room—or in the town—that Black plans ...Rh6. And he plays it—in three moves. Why not now? That his Bishop is attacked doesn't bother him. It is still attacked three moves hence.

No—what grabs his attention are the captures, the pawn-and-Rook exchanges. Players often have a hard time ordering priorities when a capture is possible. There's a compulsion to make the exchange, *then* get on with life. But a capture is *just another move.* All moves lead to new positions to be judged. Black can play *...ab4* or *...Rh6* or *...Kh8* or *...Nd3* or *...a4* or ...

He should resist the impulse to grab the b-pawn, and just look for the best move.

Be Politically Correct—when picking a piece to do a job, be an equal opportunity employer. Give no preferences to a move that "takes."

**analysis (after 14... Rh3)**

I think *14... Rh6* wins and *14... ab4* loses.

After *14... Rh6,* there are a *lot* of black pieces in the vicinity of the white King. Makes you think there should be something.... *15. h3 Bxh3!* Now it's mate if *16. gh3,* and *...Bxg2* is the threat, so *16. g3□* ... but ah, that's *two* weakening pawn moves—*16... Rg6* (△ *...Rxg3†*) *17. Nf4 Bxe3! 18. fe3 (18. Nxg6*

*Qxg3†) Rxg3† 19. Kf2 Rg2#.*

But alas, instead ...

| 14. | ... | ab4? |
| 15. | ab4 | Rxa1 |
| 16. | Qxa1 | Rh6 |

And all the black attacking pieces are where we just saw them win. So what's the difference? The white Queen can now get to Black's back rank via the a-file or by way of e5—all thanks to Black.

Now, if he didn't have better White could draw with *17. Bxe5 de5 18. Qxe5 Bd6 19. Qe8† Bf8 20. Qe5 (20. h3 Bxh3) Bd6=.*

**17. h3 Rg6**

*"Black is lost! 18. Qa8! stops the perpetual check and wins material in all variations:*

*"18... Qd8 19. Ne7† Qxe7 20. Qxc8† Qf8 21. Qxf8† Kxf8 22. bc5.*

*"18... Qxh3? 19. Ne7† Kf8 (or ...Kh8) 20. Nxg6† and 21. gh3.*

*"18... Rxg2† 19. Kxg2 Qxh3† 20. Kg1 with the threat of Qxc8† followed by Ne7†.*

*"However, White miscalcu-lated—he thought he had time for …*

**18.  bc5?          Rxg2†**
**19.  Kxg2**

*"White now expected 19…
Qxh3† 20. Kg1 and expected, at the
worst, to get into perpetual check—in
which case he would still pick up some
rating points.*

*"When Black played …*

**19.  …            Bxh3†**

*"… White was surprised, and—
without much thought—instinctively
shied away from the discovered check,
so …*

**20.  Kg1??         Qg5†**
**21.  Resigns**

*"After 20. Kh2, it looks as
though Black has to settle for the
perpetual check because of the threat
of Qa8†—although the position would
bear some investigation. What do you
think?"*

—Tykodi

Shake hands. Draw.

*"A game of missed opportunities
for White."*

—Tykodi

And Black!

Mr. Reich mixes equal parts Steinitz and Barden, shakes well and makes—Shakespeare.

## w: Richard Reich (1839)
## b: Bill Williams (2262)
Ruy Lopez C93/17(89)
## 1992 WISCONSIN CHAMPIONSHIP

| 1. | e4 | e5 |
|----|-----|-----|
| 2. | Nf3 | Nc6 |
| 3. | Bb5 | |

The Ruy Lopez (**Ru**-ee Lo-**paith**), aka The Spanish Torture. Ruy Lopez de Segura (*c.* 1530-*c.* 1580) thought *2... Nc6* was a mistake because it "allowed" *3. Bb5*. Today we don't think *Bb5* is *that* strong, but this is still one of the theoretically best ways to open a chess game. *2. Nf3* attacked e5, *3. Bb5* attacks its defender, establishing our theme — pressure against e5.

Leonard Barden:

*White's attack is usually strengthened by the advance of his other centre pawns to c3 and d4. The intention is to compel Black to play ...e5xd4, after which White controls the centre and can attack on either wing. The fact that Black often defends the Lopez by a general advance of his Queen's wing's pawns, incidentally chasing away White's Bishop, leads to a second underlying idea. White's pawn at e4 is a support point for Knight outposts at d5 and f5, and Black's conventional pawn formation at c5, d6, and e5 commits him to guarding d5 and f5 with minor pieces. Much apparently slow maneuvering in this opening is focused 'round White's efforts to establish a Knight securely on one of the key outpost squares, and to use it as a pivot for attack against the black King or for an outflanking invasion with a Rook along the a-file.*

| 3. | ... | a6 |
|----|-----|-----|

Seeing that White can't win the e-pawn, since *4. Bxc6 dc6 5.*

*Nxe5 Qd4* gets one back.

Black has other third moves, but *3... a6* is most common. It gives him the option of retaining his Knight (*...b5*), should the pressure on e5 require it.

|     |        |      |
| --- | ------ | ---- |
| 4.  | Ba4    | Nf6  |
| 5.  | 0-0    | b5   |

Early. When played now, it is often followed by *6... Bb7*. But here Black transposes back to more usual lines.

|     |        |      |
| --- | ------ | ---- |
| 6.  | Bb3    | Be7  |
| 7.  | Re1    | 0-0  |
| 8.  | c3     | d6   |

Passing on the Renowned Marshall Attack — *8... d5!? 9. ed5 Nxd5 10. Nxe5 Nxe5 11. Rxe5 c6 12. d4 Bd6.*

**9. h3**

Not strictly necessary, but White finds it easier to support d4 if he does not allow *...Bg4.*

**9. ...          Re8**

A lot of moves are played here, but rarely this. *10... Re8* is often preceded by *9... h6.* Black is trying to save a move....

|     |        |      |
| --- | ------ | ---- |
| 10. | Ng5    | Rf8  |
| 11. | Nf3    |      |

Draw?

|     |        |      |
| --- | ------ | ---- |
| 11. | ...    | h6   |

No.

|     |        |      |
| --- | ------ | ---- |
| 12. | d4     | Re8  |
| 13. | Nbd2   |      |

White wants to maintain those pawns on d4 and e4 for as long as he can. They give him a space advantage and the more dynamic and plausible possibilities, e.g., *d4-d5* or *de5* or just piece play. But first he will maneuver, using his greater space to most effectively post his pieces, hoping to make one of those moves — or a direct attack — even better than it is now. His advantage is that he can sit on this pawn structure, but even if he should be forced to resolve it, both *d5* and *de5* do not damage his position, though they *may* tend toward equality.

Black's problem is that he lacks this flexibility. He would *not* want to play *...ed4;* after *c3xd4* White would have an even greater space advantage (note: he swopped c3 for e5 — a good deal!). So Black tries to be ready for all contingencies, hopes he can answer blow for blow, hopes White slips up.

| 13. | ... | Bb7 |
| 14. | Nf1 | Bf8 |
| 15. | Ng3 | Na5 |
| 16. | Bc2 | g6 |
| 17. | Qd3 | |

New? Kortchnoi gained a slight advantage versus Smyslov in 1970 on the Queenside starting with 15. (Yes, 15. No Ng5-f3, ...Re8-f8.) a4 Qd7 16. b3 Bg7 17. Bd2.

And Gheorghiu in 1965 versus Panno did about as well on the Kingside: *15. Nh2 Bg7 16. f4 ef4 17. Bxf4.*

*17. Qd3* is less direct, but seems okay. The Queen is safe enough there for the time being, covering important center squares and working toward connecting the Rooks — always a useful thing to do.

Now Black's *17... Bg7* is likewise okay, but doesn't seem immediately necessary. It looks better to either play ...c5 at once or recycle the Knight with *17... Nc4 18. b3 Nb6.* An ever-present risk Black runs is that White will close things with *b3* and *d5,* when the B/b7 and N/a5 will be out of play while white pieces converge on the other wing.

| 17. | ... | Bg7 |

| 18. | b3 | ed4 |

I think this only helps White. I like *18... c5.* If White avoids *19. d5,* Black can favorably reposition his Knight with *19... cd4 20. cd4 Nc6.* If *19. d5,* Black can profit from *17. Qd3* with *19... c4,* since *20. b4* is ruled out. Then Black can take on b3 and look for c-file play.

| 19. | cd4 | c5 |
| 20. | Bb2 | |

Isn't it indeed better for White with the pawns gone from c3 and e5?

Still, with *20... Nc6 △ ...Nb4* Black's pieces have reasonable potential.

| 20. | ... | Qb6 |
| 21. | d5 | |

Well-timed. If now *21... c4,* then *20... Qb6* turns out to be unfortunate, since White can harass it with *Bd4* after *22. Qd2,* e.g., *21... c4 22. Qd2 (△ Bc3) b4 (or 22... Bc8 23. Bc3 Nb7 24. bc4 bc4 25. Rab1* with great Queenside play — *Bd4, Ba4,*

*Re c1) 23. Bd4.*

Note that the tactical try *21... Nxe4 22. Bxg7 Nxg3 23. Bxh6* is good for White.

| 21. | ... | Rac8 |
| 22. | Qd1 | |

Both to take whatever sting there is out of ...c4 and angle for the Kingside.

Note how difficult it is to get the N/a5 to a good square.

| 22. | ... | Re7 |
| 23. | Rc1 | Rce8 |
| 24. | Ba1 | |

Perhaps to take any possible sting out of ...Nxe4?! by protecting the Bishop.

| 24. | ... | Qc7 |
| 25. | Bd3 | Bc8 |

To meet White's next.

| 26. | b4 | Nb7 |
| 27. | a3 | Qb8 |
| 28. | Bb1 | |

This is getting downright Steinitzian. Maybe next *Nh1, Nh2-f1!?*

Actually, I can guess three reasons for *28. Bb1*:

— d5 is now covered in the line *29. e5!? de5 30. bc4.*

— In a similar line, the Bishop may be good on a2.

— White's clock was ticking....

Now *29. e5* does look good, or White can think about *Nh4* with *Qf3* (and *Nhf5!?*).

| 28. | ... | Nd7 |

| 29. | Bxg7 | Kxg7 |
| 30. | Kh1 | |

Unnecessary. I like *30. Nh4*, maybe now with *f2-f4*.

But Black's game is still difficult. He needs more black pieces and fewer white ones in the vicinity of his King. He tries — I think his *30... f6* is to stop *e4-e5* in some White combination with the pressure on c5, and to prepare ...Nd8-f7.

But note how ...f6 weakens g6. How can White get things to g6?

| 30. | ... | f6?! |
| 31. | Nh4 | a5? |

He had to play *31... Nf8*, when after, say, *32. f4* Black has few good squares and an onerous defensive burden.

How *can* White get things to g6?

| 32. | Nxg6! | Kxg6 |
| 33. | e5† | Kf7 |

On *33... Kg7*, both *34. Qg4†* and *34. Nf5†* look adequate.

| 34. | Qh5† | Kf8 |

**35. Qxh6†      Rg7**

*Give me another horse!*
— King Richard the Third (Reich)
V iii 178

**36. Nf5**
Barden *did* write a book on this opening.

**36. ...      R8e7**
**37. Nxe7      Nxe5**
**38. f4      ab4**

*38... Nf7 39. Ng6† mates* next.

**39. fe5      de5**
**40. Nxc8      Resigns**

Very mature play by White. And, to his considerable credit, Black recovered to tie for first in the tournament.

"See, there is Kittsley, standing like a stone wall."
—General B. E. Bee at Bull Run

### w: Scott Kittsley (1603)
### b: Bernard Pukel (1953)
Stonewall Attack D00/4(23) or A45/4(20)
## VETERAN'S TOURNAMENT, WI, 11/5/89

| 1. | d4 | d5 |
| 2. | e3 | Nf6 |
| 3. | Bd3 | g6 |
| 4. | f4 | |

The Stonewall Attack. This setup with Black is the Stonewall Variation of the Dutch Defense. For a discussion of some ideas involved, see Game U. It is particularly effective after *1… d5*. If White shows the d4-e3-f4 pawn formation before Black has moved his d-pawn, he might well play *…d6* and deny White the thematic use of e5.

| 4. | ... | Bg7 |
| 5. | Nf3 | 0-0 |
| 6. | 0-0 | c6 |

Why? A common continuation would be *6… c5 7. c3 Nc6.* But if Black rejects *…c5*, why move the pawn at all — yet, any-

way? d5 is not attacked, and it is already defended twice. Black next plays *…Nbd7*, *…Ne8-d6*, *…f6*, etc. He could do all that with the pawn on c7.

| 7. | Ne5 | Nbd7 |
| 8. | c3 | |

Why? (The Interactive Reader can fill in the rest of this paragraph.)

| 8. | ... | Ne8 |
| 9. | Nd2 | Nd6 |
| 10. | Ndf3 | |

Probably best; but he could also reasonably play *10. e4*, when it's useful to have d4 defended, thus to a degree justifying *8. c3.* Of course, he should not play *10. e4 only* to justify *8. c3.*

| 10. | ... | f6 |
| 11. | Nxd7 | Bxd7 |
| 12. | Bd2 | Qc8 |

To trade his bad Bishop for White's good one. It is the more locked pawns that determine a Bishop's virtue. A black pawn is more likely to remain on d5 than on f6.

Meanwhile, White works to get his problem Bishop out to the business side of his pawns, though this becomes a bit delayed.

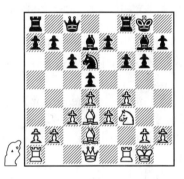

| 13. | Be1 | Bf5 |
| 14. | h3 | Qe6 |

A little awkward, as ...e6 or ...e5 will likely soon be called for. He could play *14... Bxd3 15. Qxd3 Ne4*, or simply *14... Be4*, when the Bishop is "bad" in name only. In either case, a way to activate the troops could be ...e6, ...Rf7-c7, ...Bf8, ...c5, not necessarily in that order, e.g., *14... c5!?*

| 15. | Bf2 | Bxd3 |
| 16. | Qxd3 | Nc4? |

Giving White a fairly useful free move. Better *16... Ne4* or *16... Qe4*. Black has a small advantage, because of that great outpost and better long-term Bishop prospects. In general, he should not resist exchanges, and should favor putting his pawns on light squares, keeping white pawns on dark ones. That's the specific problem with *16... Nc4* — it encourages White to lighten up his pawns.

| 17. | b3 | Nd6 |
| 18. | Rac1 | b5 |
| 19. | g4 | Ne4 |
| 20. | Nd2 | h5 |

Double-edged. Doubled e-pawns reduce his flexibility but cover d3 and f3, somewhat restricting White.

| 21. | Nxe4 | de4 |
| 22. | Qe2 | hg4 |
| 23. | Qxg4 | |

I think *23. hg4* is better, but Black makes *23. Qxg4* work out, as will be discussed.

| 23. | ... | f5! |
| 24. | Qg2 | Kf7 |
| 25. | Bh4 | |

And this comes to a good end, but I think the Bishop's future would be more reliably assured by *Be1* and *c3-c4*.

| 25. | ... | Rh8 |
| 26. | Bg5 | |

**26. ...          Bf6?!**

No, no. This Bishop is still the better one, even though the white Bishop has increased its activity. And see the pawn on h3? In two moves, it will be on g5. That can't be right.

White has committed some resources to the Kingside. Black should hold the fort there (he has an "extra" useful piece — the King) and open a line on the Queenside. *26... a5, 27... a4* allows the blocking *28. b4,* so I suggest *26... Rac8.* If then *27. b4, 27... a5!* and *...Ra8.* Otherwise, *27... c5.* White would likely not play *d4xc5* — after *...Rxc5* his c-pawn would be weak and the B/g7 a tiger. Black would not hurry *...c5xd4,* but set it up with *...Rc6* (also covering g6!) and *...Rhc8, maybe ...a5,* then *...cd4* or *...c4* or *...a4,* depending on what White has been up to.

Handled correctly, I think Black's initiative is more danger-ous than White's, at least enough to compel White to shift to Queenside defense. And that would allow Black to safely move his Queen and play *...e6* and *...Bf8,* when the difference in Bishops could be decisive, both in attacking pawns and control-ling squares.

**27. h4          Bxg5?**

*No, no ...*

For the theoretical reasons just discussed. And for a practical one. Play *27... Rh4.* Do you think White will play *Bxf6?* It ain't likely! After *...Qxf6* and *...Rah8,* he welcomes your sug-gestions on defending h4. Do you think White will make any other Bishop move?

Heh, heh, heh.

So why take a piece that ain't gonna move?! Try *27... Rh5 28. Kf2 Rah8 29. Rh1.* Now White must cover that Rook with the Queen and the other Rook. And he can't move the Bishop.

Meanwhile, Black's Bishop and Rooks are doing fine; let's activate the Queen. *29... a5 30. Kg3* (see anything more useful? If *30. Rcg1, 30... a4.* And, in any event, Black can at the last safe moment play *...Bxg5,* sealing the g-file) *a4 31. b4* (say) *Qc4,* or *31... Bxg5 32. hg5 Qc4,* and it's suddenly a wolf among the sheep.

And there are other plans.

Instead of *31… Qc4*, Black could go the other way — *…Kg7, …R8h7, …Qg8!, …Qh8*. And in any variation he probably has time to play his King to a6 if that seems a good idea — and move it back if it doesn't.

*Or … but you get my point.*

| 28. | hg5 | Rh4 |
| 29. | Kf2 | Rah8 |
| 30. | Rh1 | Qc8 |

Black still has a slight initiative, but he does not have the weaknesses in White's camp that he might have induced.

*30… Rg4? 31. Rxh8 Rxg2†*
*32. Kxg2 is better for White.*

| 31. | Rxh4 | Rxh4 |
| 32. | Rh1 | Qh8 |
| 33. | Rxh4 | Qxh4† |

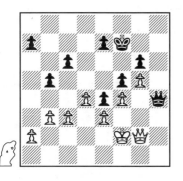

| 34. | Kf1 | Qh5?! |

A position neither side can win, either side could lose.

In some pawn endings, White would have an advantage because of Black's doubled pawns; but Black has the activity advantage *now* to avoid that.

For White to try to win, he must penetrate with his Queen, probably by playing *c3-c4*, while avoiding a perpetual. To indeed avoid that, he must get his King away from the Kingside (e.g., *35. Qe2? Qh1† 36. Kf2 Qh2†* would draw at once, since White can't allow *37. Ke1? Qg1† 38. Kd2 Qb1*). So *34… Qh5* only helps White. Black should play *34… Ke6* at once.

| 35. | Ke1 | Ke6 |
| 36. | Kd2 | Kd5 |
| 37. | Qe2 | |

Now Black can grab a draw. After *37… Qxe2† 38. Kxe2 a5 39. Kd2 (39. a3? a4 40. ba4 ba4 41. Kd2 Kc4 42. Kc2 e6!−+) c5*, White can't do better than allow a block with *40. Kc2 a4 41. Kb2*, since any *d4xc5* would allow Black to undouble his pawns with a later *…e5*. Then Black could create a counter-balancing passed pawn of his own.

But an extraneous factor enters the mix — the 350-point rating difference. Black feels "materially" obliged to play for a win. And the tournament situation may encourage that.

| 37. | … | Qh1 |
| 38. | Qe1 | Qh8 |

*38… Qg2† 39. Qe2 Qg1 40. Qe1 Qg2† is equal.*

| 39. | Qe2 | a6 |
| 40. | c4† | Kd6 |

**41. c5†?!**

As was the case with *27... Bxg5?*, there's no need to hurry with this, since White need not fear *...bc4*. He could perhaps more usefully play *41. Kc2*.

**41. ... Kd5**

**42. a3**

Threatening *b4, Kc3, Qa2 mate!*

**42. ... Qh1**

**43. Qe1 Qxe1†**

*43... Qg2†* would not worry me....

**44. Kxe1 a5**

**45. Kd2 a4??**

*Arrrgh!*

Well, he avoids the draw. *45... b4=*, as White's King is denied d3, c3, a3.

**46. Kc3**

*46. ba4* also wins. *Black* wins *46. b4? Kc4 47. Kc2 e6*. If that's what he was playing for, submit his name to The Optimists' Hall of Fame.

**46. ... ab3**

**47. Kxb3 Ke6**

No better is *47... e5 48. de5 Kxc5 49. Kc3 Kd5 50. Kb4 c5† 51. Kxb5 c4 52. Kb4*.

**48. Kb4 Kd7**

**49. Ka5 Kc7**

**50. Ka6 e6**

We may have a world record here; this is very late for the first move of an e-pawn. I'll check with Tim Krabbé. He knows this stuff....

**51. Ka7 Kc8**

**52. Kb6 Kd7**

**53. Kb7 e5**

**54. de5 Resigns.**

## PART III — Pawn Play and Weak Squares

Two sides of the same coin—Pawn moves leave weak squares behind. But you must move some Pawns! The trick is to minimize the weaknesses—or more to the point—to make sure that when you accept them you reap counterbalancing benefits. Every weakness has its price.

Archimedes said if you gave him a lever long enough and a place to stand he could move the earth. Mr. Millett says if you give him a single square he can win a game. Not sure which is more impressive.

**w: Philip Millett (2098)**
**b: Charles Gumienny (2190)**
Pirc Defense B08/31(158)
## 11TH US CC CH. PRELIM

| | | | | |
|---|---|---|---|---|
| 1. | e4 | d6 | 4. ... | Bg7 |
| 2. | d4 | Nf6 | 5. Be2 | 0-0 |
| 3. | Nc3 | g6 | 6. 0-0 | |
| 4. | Nf3 | | | |

The Classical System, one of the two most common ways of meeting the Pirc (pron. *Peerts*) Defense. The other is *4. f4*, the Austrian Attack. Neither is theoretically better than the other, but the Austrian has sharper, more critical variations, with White often going for a quick attack with *e4-e5*.

In the Classical White adopts a more modest pawn center, and more modest ambitions. But Black must not be any less alert. The white pieces can be dangerous indeed in the hands of a player skilled in nursing a small advantage.

Now Black has two main choices — 6... *Bg4* and 6... *c6*. The latter is more flexible, planning ...*b5* or ...*d5* or ...*Qc7* and ...*e5*. It avoids early exchanges and tends toward slightly less symmetrical positions. But it *is* often a little cramped.

6... *Bg4* is more direct, playing against the d4-square with Moves 6, 7, and 8.

| 6. | ... | Bg4 |
|---|---|---|
| 7. | Be3 | Nc6 |
| 8. | Qd2 | e5 |

John Nunn —

*After 8... e5 White can play 9. de5 or 9. d5, these two moves leading to quite different positions. White's aim with 9. de5 is to preserve a slight endgame advantage while avoiding any chance of defeat. 9. d5 is probably no better for White, but leads to more interesting positions.*

But that depends on what interests you.

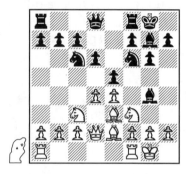

| 9. | de5 | de5 |
|----|-----|-----|
| 10. | Rad1 | Qxd2 |

An interesting choice by a strong player in a correspondence game. Both *ECO* and Nunn's *The Complete Pirc* show equality after *10... Qc8 11. Qc1 Rd8 12. Rxd8† Qxd8 (12... Nxd8!? –Nunn) 13. Rd1 Qf8 14. h3 Bxf3 15. Bxf3 h5 (△ ...Kh7 and ...Bh6).*

Perhaps Black feared a White improvement? Or thought he had one in the game line? Or felt it was more double-edged, if riskier? (Or — *ah!* — perhaps he needs more fine books from CHESSCO!)

| 11. | Rxd2 | Rfd8 |
|-----|------|------|
| 12. | Rfd1 | Rxd2 |

| 13. | Rxd2 | Ne8 |
|-----|------|-----|

Defending e5 so that his other Knight can support ...Rd8.

Now *ECO* gives lines with *14. Nd5* and *14. h3*, but suggests *14. Bb5* as "!?".

Nunn gives *14. Bb5* "!" — "... and White is clearly better, e.g., *14... Bxf3 15. Bxc6* or *14... Ne7 15. Bxe8 Rxe8 16. Nb5.*"

| **14.** | **Bb5!?/!** | **Nd6!?** |
|---------|-------------|-----------|

Black improves (?) on Nunn's first line, accepting the doubled pawns but retaining his good Bishop. But is this good enough for equality?

| **15.** | **Bxc6** | **bc6** |
|---------|----------|---------|

These pawns are weaker than doubled pawns on f2 and f3 would be, because they are doubled *and* isolated — no pawn support in sight. After *16... Bxf3 17. gf3* White can work to get in an eventual *f4*, when the pawns abreast function well, and undoubling may take place.

How serious is Black's problem? The c-pawns *are* weak, but it is not easy for White to get at them, e.g., there's no convenient way to attack c6. The trouble is not so much weak pawns as weak squares, especially c5. It's a great comfort to have places to sit where you are safe from irritation by pesky pawns. This may not immediately result in gain for White, but as his options increase, Black's tend to decrease. A Bad Sign.

Black's answer? Activity. Centralization. Attention to specifics.

Now White stops ...Nc4. He sure doesn't want to give up another Bishop.

| 16. | b3 | f6 |
|-----|-----|-----|
| 17. | Ne1 | Bf8 |
| 18. | Nd3 | |

With the idea Nb4 Bd7; Na4-c5-a6. Weak squares!

| 18. | ... | Nb5 |

He did not want to do this when White could respond Nxb5 cb5; Rd5.

Now, of course, White does not straighten out Black's pawns with 19. Nxb5? cb5, but heads for, yep, c5.

| 19. | Na4 | Rd8 |
| 20. | f3 | Bc8 |

Were there no Queenside pawn problems (e.g., slide c7 to b6), Black might well play 20... Be6.

| 21. | c3 | |

Wondrous Calm. He takes squares away and dares Black to make a move. There aren't many, e.g., 21... Kf7? 22. Nxe5†. It's ugly, but I think Black should play 21... g5, then 22... Be7, ...Kf8-e8.

He plays 21... Be7 immediately, and it makes a huge difference in the position! Because now suddenly good is ...

| 21. | ... | Be7 |
| 22. | c4! | |

Extraordinary. First, the easy stuff — if 22... Nd6 or ...Na3(?), 23. Bxa7. So Black plays the obvious ...

| 22. | ... | Nd4 |
| 23. | f4 | |

And the trouble is that there's no good way to cover e5 (23... Bd6, yep, 24. c5).

23... ef4 costs the a-pawn after 24. Nxf4 Ne6 25. Rxd8†.

So how did 21... Be7 change things? Without that move, Black could now play 23... Bh6!, easing the attack on e5 by pinning the f-pawn and allowing the N/d4 time to withdraw with Honor. Best (?) seems 24. Kf2 ef4 25. Nxf4 Ne6. It's tricky, but I think Black's okay.

| 23. | ... | Ne2† |

Black gives it his best (practical) shot.

| 24. | Rxe2 | Rxd3 |
| 25. | fe5 | Bg4 |

25... fe5 26. Bxa7.

But the text looks good. If 26. Re1, 26... Bb4 embarrasses White.

**26. ef6          Bxe2**

About (?) as good for White is 26... Bb4 27. Kf2! Bxe2 28. Kxe2, when those two passed pawns are worth more than an exchange, as would become especially clear when the Knight becomes centralized.

**27. fe7          Kf7**
**28. Kf2          Bg4**
**29. h3**

White has calculated well indeed, seeing that he has this and his next move to chase the Rook back before covering e7.

**29. ...          Bc8**
**30. Ke2**

**30. ...          Rd7?!**

Surely White's 31. Bc5 may be anticipated. Black could get a slightly better version of the game with 30... Rd6 31. Bc5 Bd7 (31... Kxe7? 32. e5), or he could keep his Rook with 31... Re6,

when White has the happy choice between 32. Ke3 and 32. Nc3! Have I mentioned the c5-square?

Bagging a7 probably wins too.

**31. Bc5          Rd6**
**32. e8=Q†**

32. Ke3 is okay, but White sees a clear win with the text.

**32. ...          Kxe8**
**33. Bxd6          cd6**
**34. c5**

Ahem. The point is to nail Black's c-pawn on the color of his Bishop.

**34. ...          Ke7**
**35. Ke3          g5**
**36. cd6†          Kxd6**
**37. Kd4**

Controlling, er, c5.

Now Black's ...h5, ...h4, ...g4 is his best chance. It helps get his longer-range piece swooping room, and the fewer pawns, the better — one versus none could draw! But White can avoid that easily enough.

**37. ...          h5**
**38. Nc5          h4**

38... g4? 39. hg4 and 40. g3 limits exchanges. But that's a picky point — with those pawns gone, White still wins without trouble.

**39. b4          g4**
**40. hg4          Bxg4**
**41. Nd3          Be2**

42.  Nf4        Bf1

43.  a3

Perhaps an over-refinement, but very nice. Good in general, of course, because of the square color; but it also is a bit *zugzwangical*. Black can't move the Bishop (*44. Ng6*), and so must play *43... Kd7* (*...Ke7 44. Ng6†*) or *43... a6*. Both moves concede squares: if *43... a6*, White would play *44. Ng6 Bxg2 45. Nxh4 Bf1*, when *46. Nf5† Kd7 (-e6) 47. Kc5* and *48. Nd6* wins; if Black had played *43... Kd7*, White could go for something like that, or try to run the e-pawn with *46. Ke5*.

Instead, Black has a little joke; but White didn't come this far to leave something relatively simple uncalculated.

43.  ...        Bxg2
44.  Nxg2      h3
45.  Ne3       Resigns.

Mr. Ziegler's smile bring sunshine.

## w: Max Lawrence
## b: Cliff Ziegler

English Opening A07/14

### CAISSA's PAGEANT cc. 1979

| 1. | c4 | Nf6 |
|----|-----|------|
| 2. | g3 | c6 |
| 3. | Nf3 | d5 |
| 4. | b3 | Bg4 |
| 5. | Bg2 | Nbd7 |
| 6. | Bb2 | e6 |

Fine. A little unambitious. In variations of this and similar openings, ...Bg4 is played with the idea ...Bxf3 and ...e5.

But here, Black simply wanted his "bad" Bishop out of the c6-d5-e6 diocese. There's a lot to be said for excommunication. It may not be a perfect solution, but it sure clarifies an issue.

| 7. | 0-0 | Bd6 |
|----|-----|------|
| 8. | d3 | Bxf3 |

Not as bad as it looks. Faint Praise Department. Black plays this before White has time for *Nbd2xf3*. A Knight is better than a Bishop on f3; it can often profitably go to e5 or d4 and it deters ...Ne5, while a Bishop functions about as well on g2 as on f3 — and on f3 it is subject to attack by ...Ne5, when it would "have" to move again. So Black hopes he's not wasting a whole move by not waiting for *h2-h3*.

| 9. | Bxf3 | 0-0 |
|----|------|------|
| 10. | Nd2 | |

*10. Nc3* looks better. *10... d4* would cause White to lose time with his Knight, but Black would have to spend as much or more time moving his e-pawn and/or c-pawn a second time to cover d4. Then *e2-e3* would open the position for White's two Bishops.

After *10. Nd2* Black has several likely continuations. Best may be playing in the center with

10... Re8 and ...e5. If White doesn't contest that setup, Black can sit on it, finish developing (e.g., ...Qe7, ...Rad8), and perhaps look at ...e4 (...e3!). That possibility is one reason I prefer 10. Nc3; it would be harder for Black to carry out with the added White pressure on d5.

In his notes to the game, Black said he felt White's dark-square Bishop was better than his own. That being the case, he could have played 10... Be5, when White must exchange his Queen's Bishop or block it in with 11. d4.

Instead, Black tries to swop Bishops on a3.

**10. ...        Qa5**

Mr. Ziegler: "Black's ...Qa5 may not be the perfect answer in this position; but it has a specific objective, and with White's help could lead to a better position. Chess however, that is good chess, does not thrive on hope, it thrives on the specifics of a position. (But) White now proceeds to help Black acquire a fine game."

**11. a3        b5**

Mr. Ziegler: "As I look at this move now 14 years later, I don't like it. It works fine, but don't blame me. Instead of the move White plays it seems cd5 or cb5 would be better. His Bishops

have more scope. But he chooses rather to drive Black backwards, and in the process puts his Queen's Bishop out of play."

Mr. Ziegler is doubtless correct that White misplays this, and that cb5 (say) is better. But it may not be best. And certainly not now — if 11. cb5 cb5 12. b4, Black has the convenient 12... Qb6.

White should play as in the game, when Black can't play 12... Qb6? 13. c5. Black plays 12... Qd8 with the game continuation in mind. It works fine. Don't blame him.

**12. b4        Qd8**

*"Can we talk pawns?"*
— Joan Rivers

The suggested 13. cb5 is indeed okay. After 13... cb5, White has various active setups — Nb3-d4 or Bd4-c5 or Bd4, Nc5; or if 14... e5, Rc1, Nb3-a5, Qb3, with play versus d5, c6, b7. White has an edge, but I think

Black holds with ...e5, ...Qb6, ...Rac8. Opposing Rooks on the open file have a neutralizing effect.

Let's look at the diagram again. Look at what *13. cb5 cb5 did.* Removed the pawns on c4 and c6. So what? Aren't all pawns created equal? They come off the *lathe* equal maybe, but early training, nutrition, edumacation, quality day care, etc., result in pawns as different as you and me. Look at those pawns on c4 and c6. Look at what each can do. Pawn/c4 can take on b5, take on d5, or advance to c5. Pawn/c6 ... is disadvantaged. Not his fault, but his prospects just don't compare.

Trading c4 for c6 is like trading a .300-hitter for a bench warmer.

White should probably play *13. Rc1,* then *Nb3* or *Qb3* and double Rooks. If Black captures on c4, the open lines all seem to lead to The Underprivileged One on c6. He could try to Advance in Life, but lacks the early preparation, e.g., *13. Rc1 bc4 14. dc4 c5* — admirable pluck, but — *15. Bxf6 Nxf6 16. bc5 Bxc5 17. cd5....*

### 13.   c5?

Like an honor student turned to crime, his future is now hardly brighter than the waif's on c6.

| 13. | ... | Be5 |
| 14. | d4?! | |

And this is about as bad. Mr. Ziegler quotes from an obscure tome, *Journal of a Chess Master,* doubtless Long out of print, to wit, "The important thing is to adjust the position to suit *your* pieces." White isn't doing that. He voluntarily has given himself a *bad* Bishop on b2.

Instead, he should play *14. Qc2, Bg2, Nf3* or *14. Bxe5 Nxe5 15. Bg2 △ e3, Qe2, f4,* in both cases with approximate equality.

| 14. | ... | Bc7 |
| 15. | e4 | |

I think White should admit he made a mistake and try to repair the damage, rehabilitating his Bishop by *Bg2, Nf3, Bc1-g5.*

He might try *15. a4 △ 15... ba4?! 16. Qxa4 Nb8 17. b5,* rehabilitating the Promising One on c5. But Black can play simply *15. a4 a6* or *15... Qb8!?,* when White must block with *16. a5* or suffer a weak b4 on an open file.

The text move is well-motivated, trying to advance and penetrate — but look at the pawns when d5 and e4 come off. The d5-square is an ideal Knight post, safe from pawn harassment and even shielding c6. White has no such safe square. Such a pawn setup would be acceptable for White if he had accompanying advantages — play on the e-file, say, or prospects for a Kingside attack. But Black can hold the important e-squares, and he can create Queenside threats so quickly that White does not have a free hand elsewhere.

White might have tried to play *e2-e4 and* control d5 by *Bg2, f3, e4,* but after *15. Bg2 a5 16. f3* Black could strike first in the center with *16... e5!,* when the resulting pawn formations are all good for Black.

Indeed, in general note the inflexibility — the lack of options — that has resulted from *13. c5?* and *14. d4?!* As Black says, don't blame him.

| 15. | ... | de4 |
| 16. | Nxe4 | Nd5 |
| 17. | Qd2 | |

White would like a black pawn on d5, both to shield d4 and deny Black his d5 piece post (decidedly not a peace post). But if *17. Nc3, 17... N7f6* and Black will keep recapturing on d5 with pieces.

| 17. | ... | a5 |
| 18. | Bg2 | |

White attempts to play on the Kingside, but I don't think he can get a preponderance of force over there. Certainly, his plan to push the f-pawn seems more loosening than threatening. *And* the Bishop does not do much on

g2.

Better looks *18. Rfb1, Bc3, Bd1,* with ideas of *a3-a4* or *Bc2* and *Ng5,* depending on Black's play. Another point in favor of *Bd1* is keeping a black Rook out of a4.

| 18. | ... | ab4 |
| 19. | ab4 | Qb8 |
| 20. | f4 | Rxa1 |
| 21. | Rxa1 | Qb7 |
| 22. | Nf2 | |

Heading for the fine d3-square. That *is* a point in favor of *20. f4,* but I still like the above plan.

Now for Black I like *22... N7f6!,* then *...Ra8.*

| 22. | ... | Ra8 |

Because now White could play (the ugly) *23. Bxd5 ed5 24. Qe1 (△ Qe7) Kf8 25. Rxa8 Qxa8 26. Qa1.* The ending *would* be grim for him with all those pawns on dark squares, but that's how bad I think his game is, that his drawing chances might be better there than here.

And better than White's passive *23. Ba3?* would be *23. Nd3* or *23. Bf3* or *23. Rxa8?!*

| 23. | Ba3? | N7f6 |
|-----|------|------|
| 24. | Bf3 | Ra6 |
| 25. | Nd3 | Qa8 |
| 26. | Qc1 | g6 |

White is pretty well tied up on the Queenside; Black looks to another front.

| 27. | Kg2 | Kg7 |
|-----|------|------|
| 28. | Kf2 | h5 |
| 29. | h3 | |

The Famous Bad Move in a Difficult Position. White weakens his Kingside pawn chain. If he left his pawn on h2 or stopped ...h5-h4 with *29. h4*, Black could increase the pressure on White's game with ...*Ng8-e7-f5*, then either ...*Bd8-f6* or ...*Qb8* looking at Knight sacks or ...*f6* and ...*g5* — all subject to White's activities.

A different 29th move would leave h2 covering g3. *29. h4* would save g3 from ...*h4*. *29. h3* is like taking the pawn off the board as far as g3 is concerned.

| 29. | ... | Qb8 |
|-----|------|------|
| 30. | Ne5 | Qa8 |
| 31. | Qb2? | |

Abandons f4. Now he can't meet *31... h4* with *32. g4*.

It's hard to say where White's game goes from bad to lost. But the Message is easy — avoid the passive and fundamentally flawed structure of *13. c5, 14. d4, 23. Ba3*. Have the Simple Faith that nothing bad can happen if your pieces can function as Caissa intended — actively, enjoying a variety of healthful exercises in fresh air and sunshine.

| 31. | ... | h4 |
|-----|------|------|
| 32. | Qb3?! | |

Deep Shade — now the Queen can't cover f4, and a4 is safe from *Bd1*.

Now Black punches left, right, left.

| 32. | ... | hg3† |
|-----|------|------|
| 33. | Kxg3 | Ra4! |

Excellent! He threatens *34... Nxb4*, or even *34... Rxb4*. So White must cover that square, but ...

| 34. | Nd3 | Bxf4†! |
|-----|------|------|
| 35. | Nxf4 | Qb8 |

Delightful. The Queen has enjoyed great scope shuffling around in this corner. The Sun doesn't always shine just in the center of the board.

But now it appears that

White's Queen *can* cover f4 by playing *36. Bxd5* and *37. Qf3!*

Nay, nay. Black has two ways to win after *36. Bxd5*:

*36... Nh5†* and wherever the King goes, Black can capture on f4 with *check*, and then recapture on d5.

*36... Nxd5 37. Qf3 g5! 38. Qg4 Qxf4† 39. Qxf4 (39. Kg2? Ne3†) gf4†* with an easy win (e.g., *...Nxb4-c2*), especially since the Bishop is *still* bad.

There is almost always a tactical solution like this when one side is passively defending weak points and the other has more active — and unhampered — pieces.

| 36. | Bb2 | Qxf4† |
| 37. | Kg2 | Qd2† |
| 38. | Resigns | |

One game got into the book as soon as I saw the winner's name. This wasn't it. This passed the test.

### w: Bob Long (1945)
### b: Bob Beelman (1895)
French Defense C02/15
## DES MOINES OPEN 1993

| 1. | d4 | e6 |
|----|-----|-----|
| 2. | e4 | d5 |
| 3. | e5 | |

Probably the most theoretically interesting move. White immediately seizes the space Black ceded with his first move.

| 3. | ... | c5 |
|----|-----|-----|
| 4. | c3 | Nc6 |
| 5. | Nf3 | Qb6 |

Thematic play against the base of White's pawn chain. Black often follows up with ...cd4 and ...Nh6(-e7)-f5. White has various ways to continue, e.g., Be2, Nc3-a4 (after ...cd4, cd4) or a3, b4, Bb2, or others. See ECO C02 or—better—a collection of Nimzovitch's games.

**6.    Bd3**

Again the most interesting move. Of course, this is the opinion of a Scribe Sitting Safely in his Study.

What do you do if you are Black and your clock is ticking? Do you go after the d-pawn? The player in this game probably considered it playable to do so, but what if you did not? Concrete analysis can give an absolute answer, of course, but that can be impossible, impractical, or unlikely.

So what do you do? Analyze the best that circumstances allow, naturally, but what of General Considerations? You must judge the value of the pawn versus the time lost, the opponent's lead in development. Time you can judge by number of pieces out, pawn worth by closeness to the center. If you grab an a-pawn or b-pawn you may win as a result, but it will likely be because the pawn plus told in the *long* run. But if, as here, you bag d4 (and e5?), it will benefit you in more ways than materially. You will have more good squares for your pieces, and perhaps the ability to advance your center pawns.

    **6.  ...          Bd7**

Black temporizes, then transposes into the line with the more usual move order 6... cd4 7. cd4 Bd7 8. 0-0 Nxd4. He must play ...Bd7 anyway if he wants to win the d-pawn. If he does not, White would win the unprotected black Queen on d4 with *Bb5 check.*

    **7.  0–0        cd4**
    **8.  cd4        Nxd4**
    **9.  Nxd4      Qxd4**
    **10.  Nc3**

Consistent, offering the second pawn, hoping to play Starry-Eyed Idealist to Black's Clutching Materialist. And anyway, it's hard to both hold e5 and drive the black Queen from its dominating position. Indeed, in the game Natapov–Karlsson 1972, after *10. Re1 Ne7 11. Nc3 a6* White didn't see better than *12. Ne2 Qxe5,* continuing *13. Bf4 Qf6 14. Qb3* "unclear."

Now we have one of the few cases in this book where I endorse a purely defensive pawn move. That's probably why Publisher Long submitted this game—just to see if I would do it. And yes, I think Black should play *10... a6.* Otherwise, *Nb5* is just too strong, with threats against c7 and d6. And if ...*BxNb5,* Black's King gets stuck in the center.

    **10.  ...         Qxe5**
    **11.  Re1       Qb8**

It takes some calculation here—or some knowledge—but this appears best, even though it allows White to recover one pawn at once (with *12. Nxd5*).

If instead Black plays *11... Qd6,* he loses more time with Queen or King after *12. Nb5* when:

*12... Qb8* has held the pawn, but allows White great activity with *13. Qf3 (△ Bf4) Bd6 14. Qxd5! Bxh2† 15. Kh1 Bc6 16. Qg5±* (Pachman). The editor looked at *16... g6 17. f4! h6 18. Qg4 h5!? 19. Qg5 a6 20. Nd4 Qd6 21. Nxe6±;* or

*12... Bxb5 13. Bxb5† Kd8*, when White has compensation with *14. g3* (or *14. Be3!?* or *14. Qf3*) *Qb4 15. a4 Bd6 16. Bd2 Qxb2 17. Rc1* (Barcza), e.g., △ *18. Ba5† b6 19. Qxd5! ed5? 20. Re8#*.

**12. Nxd5 Bd6**

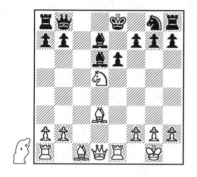

Now Bisguier played *13. Qh5?!* versus Westerinen in 1971. The trouble with the move is that after *13... Kf8* White must retreat his Knight—*14. Nc3*. But that allows Black to develop with tempo, and he was slightly better after *14... Nf6 15. Qh4 Bc6 16. Bg5 Be5*.

*13. Qg4* is much better. A big point is that it pins the e-pawn another way, so that after *13... Kf8* White need not retreat his Knight. After then *14. Bd2* ECO leaves us with "with compensation for the material." Mr. Long continues this line with *14... f5* (in Gambit-Grabbing Style. Perhaps *14... Nf6!?* or *...Nge7!?*) *15. Qf3 ed5 16. Bxf5 Bxh2†*

(Black has enough material; he should hurry pieces out with *16... Bxf5 17. Qxf5† Nf6*. After the text, he's losing, not so much because he loses his Bishop as that *Bb4†* becomes crushing.) *17. Kh1* (*17. Rxe6!?*) *Bxf5 18. Qxf5† Nf6 19. g3 Bxg3 20. fg3 Qxg3 21. Bb4† Kf7 22. Re7† Kf8 23. Rd7† Qd6 24. Bxd6† Ke8 25. Qe6#*.

**13. h3**

And here, Bob makes up for forcing me to applaud *10... a6!?*

We know that *13. h3* is probably not best, because we've seen how good *13. Qg4!* is. But I would question *13. h3* in any event. Why? Too slow. It is *so* much better to solve your problems by moving—improving, developing—a piece. Missing *13. Qg4*, I would reject *13. h3* in favor of *13. Qh5* or even *13. Bd2*, taking my chances with *13... Bxh2† 14. Kh1*. White's lead in development is the key to the position. I would like to press it, try to rush ahead as in the last note.

Unfortunately, there's no hard-and-fast rule on deciding when you should spend (waste? invest?) time on such as *13. h3*. It depends on how open a position is, how important speed. It's like stopping to tie your shoelace in a foot race. In a 100-yard dash, you obviously would not; in a marathon, you surely would. Not in a half-mile, not in a fast mile, but in a 5K? A 10K?

How do we learn this? Analysis and experience. Study Morphy games and Tal games and Fischer games; note the economy of effort, the maximum utilization of resources. And check your own games for cases where you failed to push the pace versus your opponent, allowed him to catch his breath, to tie *his* shoelace.

Helpful Hint Department: When you have an attacking position, list your candidate moves in their order of aggression. Look at the wildest first, and if you reject it, check the second on your list, etc. Even if you don't find the best move, you will err in the "right" direction. Playing the sharpest move you dare will be in the spirit of the position, good practice for you, and the most challenging for the opponent. Thus here, if White strongly rejected *13. Qg4!* he still might have settled for *13. f4.* I'm not sure how good it is, but it shields h2 *and* puts some pressure on with the threat of *f4-f5.*

**13. ...         Bc6?!**

Much too leisurely. This move does have the point of forcing the Knight to retreat, but at the cost in time of moving a developed piece twice. I'd be tempted by *13... Nf6!?* After *14. Nxf6† gf6* the development gap has narrowed, ...gf6 adds to the black King's bulwark, and Black still has his pawn plus. *And ...Rg8, ...e5, ...Bxh3* looms as an eventual possibility—another problem with *13. h3.*

And I prefer *13... Ne7* to the text.

After *1. e4 e5 2. Nf3 Nc6 3. Bb5 a6 4. Bxc6,* Black always captures the Bishop. Why? Because with his Knight off the board, he is *aware* of the great *material* imbalance. Well, in our game the *developmental* imbalance is almost as great, and nearly as important. But players rarely treat that with the same urgency as they do recapturing a piece.

**14. Ne3         Ne7**

Now ...Nf6 is not as good as it was—the e-pawn isn't covering f5 any better than it covered d5. After *14... Nf6 15. Nf5* Black can't castle: *15... 0-0? 16. Nxd6 Qxd6 17. Bxh7†.*

But *14... Nf6,* with *15... Kf8,* might be better than the text.

**15. Qh5         h6**

*15... g6? 16. Qg5* is certainly no help.

But I'm not certain *15... h6* is

best.

I *am* certain you were waiting for me to say that.

Was Black worried about *Bxh7?* How would White get the Bishop out? And the standard objections apply:

1) Weakening. The possibility of a sac on h6 is now in the air, e.g., *16. Ng4 0-0? 17. Bxh6+-.*

2) Waste of time. While Black does nothing for his pieces, White moves forward.

I'd play *15... Ng6.* It threatens *...Nf4,* hitting h5, d3, and g2, and thus tempts White to part with one of his dangerous Bishops. True, after *16. Bxg6 fg6* Black's pawn structure is not a joy to behold; but after *17. Qg4 Bd7* it is hard for White to get his pawn back—or Black could play *17... 0-0! 18. Qxe6† Kh8,* when he has two great Bishops and *might* even get ahead in development with *...Qc7* and *...Rae8.*

White's next move threatens *17. Rxe6,* which explains why Black must, alas, fall back.

| 16. | Ng4 | Bd7 |
| 17. | Bd2 | Qd8 |
| 18. | Bc3 | Kf8 |
| 19. | Rad1 | |

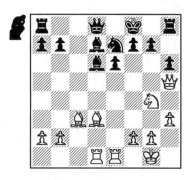

Mobilizing all of his troops. The difference in activity between the two sets of Rooks is alone almost worth a pawn.

Black's next move threatens *20... Nf4!*

| 19. | ... | Nd5 |
| 20. | Ne5 | Bxe5 |

A hard choice. All of White's pieces are dangerous, and this may be necessary. The best alternative seems *20... Be8,* holding f7 and again threatening to nab a Bishop with *21... Nf4.* But White simply plays *21. Bd2,* when *21... f6 22. Ng6† Kg8 23. Rxe6* is fine for White. And, absent that idea, it's hard to see how Black will get effectively developed, the R/h8 especially. Meanwhile, White can look to open things up with *f4-f5* or *g4-g5,* as circumstances suggest.

Black next tries to exchange Queens, or at least push White back a bit. This is well-motivated, and perhaps his best chance. But he's outnumbered.

White backs up a bit, regroups, and comes at him again.

| 21. | Bxe5 | Qg5 |
| 22. | Bd6† | Kg8 |
| 23. | Qf3 | Bc6 |
| 24. | h4! | |

Gaining space while restricting Black and reducing his options. Specifically, White wants to play Qg3. Why rob banks?

*"Because that's where the money is."*
—Willie Sutton

The black King is on the g-file.

Having decided that he wants to play *24. h4*, White must determine that it is possible. If *24... Qxh4*, White gets the game continuation with a Rook added to the mix: *25. Re4 Qf6 26. Qg3 h5 27. Be5 Qh6 28. Rh4 △ Rxh5* crunch.

| 24. | ... | Qf6 |
| 25. | Qg3 | h5 |

So he can cover g7 with his next.

| 26. | Be5 | Qh6 |
| 27. | b3! | |

Fine, resourceful play. The white and black pieces are identical, save for the B/e5 versus the N/d5. The Knight can deal with Bf4 or Bd4-e3. But a Bishop is a long-range piece; on an open board, it can use that characteristic to outflank a Knight. *27. b3!*

envisions *Bb2-c1* or perhaps *Bb2, Re5-g5*.

Black's next begins a flawed plan, but I think he's lost in any case.

| 27. | ... | Re8 |
| 28. | Bb2 | f5 |

*"This gets wood off the board, but it costs a pawn. I am not sure that 28... Nb4 would have been better because of 29. Bb1, but it doesn't lose a pawn! However, pushing my Queenside pawns will make Black miserable."*

—Long

True. And the "unopposed" Bishop threatens to dominate in that position: *30. Bc1 Qf6 31. Bg5 Qb2 (□! 31... Qa1? 32. Bh7†) 32. Rd2! Qa3(!) 33. Bf6 g6 34. Bxg6+−.*

Do you see the flaw in Black's *28... f5* idea?

| 29. | Bxf5! | |

Very nice. After *29... ef5* the black Bishop will be trying to defend both d5 and e8. How can you spot these things? Play with ideas; be aware of the potential moves of the various pieces. This is discussed at greater length in the "Inner Chess" chapter of *Journal of a Chess Master*.

| 29. | ... | ef5 |
| 30. | Rxe8† | Bxe8 |
| 31. | Rxd5 | f4 |

**32. Qc3**

Opposite-colored Bishops are drawish when pieces are few and Kings are safe; but when you're attacking, it's like having an extra piece. Thus here, when White attacks on the dark squares the black Bishop is useless in defense.

If now *32... Rh7 △ ...g6* and *...Rf7* or *...Rd7, 33. Qe5 △ Rd8* is very strong.

| | |
|---|---|
| **32. ...** | **Kh7** |
| **33. Rd6** | |

Bravo. The black Queen must cover g7; Black becomes even more congested.

| | |
|---|---|
| **33. ...** | **Bg6** |
| **34. Qc7** | **Rg8** |

Now White grabs some pawns. Fine. Wins. But more "thematically consistent" (Hanon Russell's felicitous phrase) would be *35. Bf6! Kh8 36. Bg5 Qh7* to maximize Black's congestion—admittedly, for reasons more aesthetic than practical—and then pick off some pawns.

| | |
|---|---|
| **35. Qxb7** | **f3** |

To open a line for his Queen, perhaps. And anyway, White might have played *Bc1, Rf6* (or *g2-g3*), and *Bxf4*.

| | |
|---|---|
| **36. Qxf3** | **Re8** |
| **37. Qc3** | **Re7** |
| **38. Kf1?** | |

*"Far better is 38. Bc1. Somehow I thought Black could make complications here, and I just wanted to keep the heat on. It bugs me that I thought Kf1 was better. We were getting near time control."*

—Long

Indeed, *38. Bc1* would be a fitting conclusion to the game. But now Black gets dangerously active. *Activity* is the story of this game. Note—and remember!—how on an open board, a pawn more or less is not very important if a player's pieces can freely swoop around.

| | |
|---|---|
| **38. ...** | **Qf4** |
| **39. Qg3** | |

*"I want to trade; I can win the ending. He doesn't want to trade."*

—Long

Yep. After the Queen exchange, with Rooks also off it could be drawn; but with them on, the disparate Bishops are less of a factor. And the a7-pawn is vulnerable—but not to *Ra6 Bd3†*.

| | |
|---|---|
| **39. ...** | **Qf5** |
| **40. Qg5** | **Qb1†** |
| **41. Bc1** | **Bd3†?** |

*"41... Rc7 makes White work harder."*

—Long

Rather an understatement! Doesn't that draw?! After *42. Rd1* (*Black* active, White passive!) *Qxa2*, how can White attack anything more than it can be easily (actively!) defended?

But *41... Bd3†?* returns the favor of *38. Kf1?*, and the game ends as it "should" ...

**42. Kg1          Re1†**
**43. Kh2          Bg6**

A sorry retreat. But as Mr. Long points out,

"43... Qxc1? 44. Qxh5† Qh6 (*otherwise,* 44... Kg8 45. Rd8† *puts the hammer to Black*) 45. Rxh6† gh6, *and White will have little trouble winning this because* 46. Qf7† *wins the a-pawn.*"

—Long

**44. Be3          Re2**
**45. Rd7          Resigns**

There's no defense to *46. Bd4.*

White strikes me as a player of some natural ability who perhaps has never read a chess book.

The San Antonio Chess Club News says, "Every now and then Gary Zintgraff plays like an expert on steroids.

### w: Raymond Smith (1887)
### b: Gary Zintgraff (1700)
King's Indian Defense E73
## SAN ANTONIO CC SWISS 1992

| 1. | d4 | Nf6 |
|----|-----|------|
| 2. | c4 | d6 |
| 3. | Nc3 | Nbd7 |
| 4. | e4 | e5 |
| 5. | Be3 | |

5. *Nf3* is a bit more natural, less committing. It's hard to argue that there's a better square for the Knight, but the Queen's Bishop might reasonably go to a3 or b2, d2, e3, or g5. Why decide on e3 so soon?

Black could now head toward an Old Indian with 5… *Be7*, but opts for a King's Indian.

| 5. | ... | g6 |
|----|-----|------|
| 6. | Be2 | ed4 |

Played before White plays 7. Nf3 (6. *Nf3* would have been good). White usually answers …e5xd4 with *Nxd4*. Either recapture is playable, but such cen-tralization often profits a Knight more than a Bishop.

6… *Bg7* 7. *Nf3* 0-0 would add 19 to our *ECO* code — E92/6(34).

| 7. | Bxd4 | Bg7 |
|----|------|------|
| 8. | Bf3?!/? | |

*KISS* — Keep It Simple Smith. It's hard to argue that spending three moves on *Be2*, *Bf3*, and *Nge2* is better than spending two on *Be2* and *Nf3*.

As an impromptu experiment without enough time to think it out, the move is forgivable. Give it a "?!" and move on.

But the move gets a "?" if White remembers *Bf3* (with the P/e4) being played in some positions, but didn't understand why. Most often it is seen in open Sicilians with white pawns on e4 and c2, black ones on e5 and d6. Then *Bf3* adds support to the move *Nd5*. But with pawns on e4 and c4, *Nd5* is amply supported. In King's Indian-type positions, *Bf3* most commonly appears with a black pawn on e5. I can't recall an instance in which ...*Ne5* is possible when the Bishop's retreat/protection is cut off by *Nge2*.

The Point? ***Don't try to remember moves; remember reasons for moves.***

**8.  ...          0–0**
**9.  Nge2        Re8**

White has sensitive spots on c4 and f3, as will be seen. If he deals with this by *10. Nf4 Ne5 11. Be2*, he will lose his good Bishop to *11... Nc6* because of the attack on e4.

**10.  0–0          Ne5**

The Rub. If White defends c4 — *11. b3* — he must endure *11... Nxf3† 12. gf3*, when Black has good long-term prospects with his two Bishops and better

pawns. And he may have an immediately decisive advantage. I'm not sure. But *12... Bh3 13. Re1 c5* (to avoid a Bishop exchange) *14. Be3 Nh5* △ ...*Qh4* and ...*Be5* looks dangerous. It is understandable that White prefers the text, but it actually be just as bad.

**11.  Bxe5        Rxe5**

White might have survived without his light-square Bishop, but he will sorely miss the Queen's B. He is now "weak on the dark squares." What does that mean? The pawns on c4 and e4 are more or less fixed, and with the d4-pawn gone, *and* the B/e3 gone, black pieces can flow through or land on b6, d4, f4, and especially c5 and e5. It is hard for White to cover those squares with pawns without causing further problems. Moving the b-pawn or f-pawn weakens c3 or e3. Black can get at these squares with ...c6 and ...*Qb6* or ...*Qa5*, and by putting his Bishop on g7 or h6 or maybe eventually ...*Bd4*. Even if nothing bad happens anytime soon, Black will always have the potential to jump on these squares.

**12.  Nf4          c6**

Avoiding exchanges and getting the Queen out. d6 is not hard to defend, and note — Black easily covers squares of both colors.

| 13. | Nd3 | Re8 |
| 14. | Re1 | Be6 |

If White now moves his attacked pawn — 15. c5 — Black would not bring White forward with 15... dc5?! 16. Nxc5, but invite White to bring *him* forward with 15... Bc4 16. cd6 Qxd6, when the dark-square-complex advantage is dissolving into a development, activity, two-Bishops-on-an-open-board advantage.

White finds a tactical defense by getting his Knight to e5, but

it's a short-term solution.

| 15. | e5 | de5 |
| 16. | Nxe5 | Qc7 |

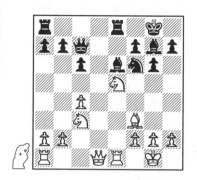

**17. Rc1**

Solving a small problem, missing a big one. White hopes

to defend c4 with *b3*, so he covers the Knight and gets his Rook off a dangerous diagonal.

The Big Problem is a little hard to see, in part because it's unusual — unlooked for. Everybody in the room sees *17... Rad8* coming. But what turns out to be important about the move is not that it attacks the Queen, but that it attacks d3. With that covered and the Queen on a4, where can the Knight go?

I think White should play *17. c5*. It makes a square for the Knight, and is even thematically pleasing — *White* fights for some dark squares. After *17... Nd5* (*17... Rad8* is also good) *18. Nxd5 Bxd5 19. Bxd5* (*19. Nd3 Rxe1† and 20... Bxf3*) *Bxe5! 20. Bb3 Bxh2†*, Black may well be winning — but the disparate Bishops offer some drawing chances. See Game T.

|     |       |        |
| --- | ----- | ------ |
| 17. | ...   | Rad8   |
| 18. | Qa4   | Bc8!   |

A remarkable winning move. The Knight is lost.

|     |       |        |
| --- | ----- | ------ |
| 19. | Nxc6  | Rxe1†  |
| 20. | Rxe1  | bc6    |
| 21. | Bxc6  | Ng4!   |

There's these dark squares, see....

|     |       |        |
| --- | ----- | ------ |
| 22. | g3    | Qb6    |

*22... Nxf2* may well work. *23. Kxf2 Bh3* sets up *...Bd4†* or *...Qb6†*. But *22... Qb6*, the Big-

gest Piece hitting the Weakest Square, can hardly be bad.

|     |       |        |
| --- | ----- | ------ |
| 23. | Re2   | Nxf2!  |

Good calculation. Or good instincts. Both are nice to have. If White does not take the Knight, Black can answer most moves (*24. Nd5* or *24. Bd5*, say) with *24... Nh3† 25. Kg2 Qg1†*, and The Industrious Reader is invited to work out the mates.

|     |       |        |
| --- | ----- | ------ |
| 24. | Rxf2  | Bxc3   |

*24... Bd4* looks good, too. But Black sees a clear forcing line.

|     |       |        |
| --- | ----- | ------ |
| 25. | bc3   | Rd2    |

How can White cover f2? By playing *Qf4!*

|     |       |        |
| --- | ----- | ------ |
| 26. | c5    | Qxc5   |
| 27. | Qf4   |        |

He even attacks d2 and f7. But the rest is easy for Black.

|     |       |        |
| --- | ----- | ------ |
| 27. | ...   | Rd1†   |
| 28. | Kg2   | Qxc6†  |
| 29. | Rf3   |        |

*29. Qf3 Qxf3† 30. Kxf3 (30. Rxf3 Bb7) Rd3† and 31... Rxc3–+.*

Now *29... Qe6* is also convincing.

|     |       |        |
| --- | ----- | ------ |
| 29. | ...   | Rd7    |
| 30. | g4    | Bb7    |
| 31. | Resigns. |     |

A little move by a little pawn on the edge of the board is enough to bring on Stroudian thunderbolts.

### w: Kevin Stroud
### b: Larry Hawkins
English Opening A18/10(46)
## USCF CLASS D POSTAL TNMT.

| | | |
|---|---|---|
| 1. | c4 | Nf6 |
| 2. | Nc3 | e6 |
| 3. | e4 | |

*3. d4* would steer us toward a Queen's Gambit or a Nimzo-Indian. *3. e4* makes it the Flohr-Mikenas Variation of the English. The most common replies are *3... c5* and the move played.

| | | |
|---|---|---|
| 3. | ... | d5 |
| 4. | e5 | d4 |
| 5. | ef6 | dc3 |
| 6. | bc3 | |

White can't win a pawn with *6. fg7* because *6... cd2* is check. But the line is certainly playable—*7. Bxd2 Bxg7 8. Qc2 Nc6 9. Nf3* is equal.

| | | |
|---|---|---|
| 6. | ... | Qxf6 |
| 7. | d4 | |

White has an advantage in the pawn-structure department. He controls a lot of center squares, and moving the pawn from b2 to c3 aids in that. These doubled pawns are more asset than liability.

Now *7... b6* and *7... c5* are most usual, but Black's choice has been played.

| | | |
|---|---|---|
| 7. | ... | Nc6 |

And one game continued 8. *Nf3 e5 9. Be2 Bf5 10. 0-0 e4 11. Ne1 Be7 12. f3 Qd6 13. fe4 Bxe4*

*14. Bf4±*, Marini–Piarzini, 1959. Different moves might reasonably be played. Brer Marini did well by developing quickly and castling. That's always a good idea. You *can* do other things, but you'd better have a good reason.

**8. c5**

I don't see the reason for this. Why is this better than getting a piece out? It stops ...Bd6, but that's not an important thing to do. Pawns on c4 and c3 covered d5 and d4. They can't do better than that. *The* four center squares are d4, d5, e4, and e5; you should have a good reason to give up control of one of them.

*If* White were fully developed—say *Nf3, Bd3, Be3, 0–0, Re1, Qd2, Rad1*—*then* he might try to rush his pawns forward.

But now his pawns are easier to attack—they have lost some flexibility, lost some options.

In fact, I like Black's play against these pawns so much that I'd advise against *8... Bxc5 9. dc5 Qxc3† 10. Bd2 Qxc5*. It's about even, but I think Black has done White a favor by removing those pawn (now) liabilities.

Black has an advantage in the pawn-structure department.

**8. ... e5**
**9. Be3 Be6**

Black could have transposed into the game with *9... ed4 10. cd4 Be6 11. Nf3*. By playing *9... Be6* at once, he tempts White to play *10. d5*, which seems to win a piece.

How does *10. d5* look to you? Should White go for this? Once I put a Rook on d8, I had my doubts. Let's play *10... 0–0–0* so *Qa4* doesn't pin the Knight. Now look at how many pieces Black has developed! And look at White's Kingside. Eight of White's ten moves have been with pawns. And now he must move another one to protect d5; *11. c4 (11. Bc4? Na5)*. Now Black can move his attacked pieces while White gets out of the pin: *11... Bf5 12. Qa4 Nd4!* Who's attacking whom? Black threatens ...Nc2†. If *13. Rc1*, ...Bxc5 stops White cold. So White takes the Knight—*13. Bxd4 ed4 14. Qxa7 d3!*, attacking a1 and threatening ...Qc3† or ...Re8† or ...d2†! And look at White's Kingside. He must be lost.

It is almost always a bad idea to attack or otherwise allow the game to open when you are so far behind in development.

**10. Nf3! ed4**
**11. cd4 Bd5!?**

Best. *11... Bg4* works on the d-pawn, but after *12. Be2* a plan involving ...Rd8 and ...Bxf3 will post White's Bishop very powerfully on f3. And once he has castled, White really might threaten *d4-d5*.

*11... Bd5!?* shows why 8. *c5* was bad. d5 is a Great Square. Black can sit on it forever. He should complete his development, ...*Be7* and ...*0-0*, then probably put his Rooks on d8 and e8. d4 will always be there to attack. That's the flexibility White lost when he played 8. *c5*.

Note the difference with Black's weakest pawn, on b7. If White attacks it, Black has a *choice*—he can defend it *or* push it, at will. And if he once plays ...*b6!?*, he can work on either c5 or d4. If White takes, *cb6 ab6*, then White's a-pawn is added to his weaknesses, while Black's now-weakest pawn, on c7, is routinely and actively defended by ...*Bd6*. Then note the difference in mobility between the B/d6 and B/e3. Black was able to gain this advantage because he did not get locked in to a pawn formation too early. He kept his options open. Let's give Mr. Marini a "!" for 8. *Nf3*.

**12. Be2 h6?!**

A bad start to a bad idea. Black wants to castle Queenside, but can't allow *Bg5* with his Rook on d8. But a better way to solve the problem—or any problem!—is to develop a piece. *12...*

*Be7* allows, if he must, *13... 0-0-0?!* while furthering development.

**13. 0-0 0-0-0?!**

It wasn't too late for *13... Be7* and *14... 0-0*, when I think Black has a slight edge. Now, he's in great danger. White has the open b-file and a Queen and King's Bishop leaning left ...

**14. Qa4**

**14. ... a6?**

If ...*h6?!* doesn't kill ya, then ...*a6* will. Black is now surely lost.

(1) *Don't move the pawns in front of your King, ever.*

(2) ... unless you have to.

If you can, remember (1) and (2). If you can only remember one of them, make it (1).

One problem with *14... a6?*, we'll see in the game. Another is the possibility of *Bxa6 ba6*, *Qxa6†*. It doesn't work now, but it's one more thing Black must now take into account.

Why did Black play it? Probably, he saw that White could play *Bb5* or *Ne5* and remove the Knight. Then he would threaten *Qxa7*. But *14… Kb8* would be a less committing way to cover a7.

And anyway, a7 is not the problem; b7 is! How can White attack a7 twice? But he *can* pile up on b7—that's on the open file. And if he does pile up on it, it *could* become vital for Black to play …b6. With the pawn on a7, he can do that; but not now.

What should he play? *14… Kb8*, and after *15. Rab1* I think Black can meet White's immediate threats—*16. Ne5 Bxc5!* *17. Ng4 Qg6* and *16. Ba6 b6*—and can try *15… Be7* or perhaps *15… g5*.

White has a big advantage, but Black may survive.

| 15. | Rab1 | Be4 |
| 16. | Rxb7! | |

Bravo! The most dramatic way to demonstrate the folly of *14… a6*. Now *16… Kxb7 17. Bxa6† Kb8 18. Qb5†* is curtains.

| 16. | … | Nb8 |

Otherwise, White takes a6. Black has no defense. White finds the sharpest denouement.

| 17. | Rxb8† | Kxb8 |
| 18. | Bxa6 | |

Here we have a classic case of overwork. Black's Bishop is trying to cover both b1 and b7. Thus White's threat is *19.*

*Rb1†!*, since *19… Bxb1* allows *20. Qb5†* to win.

| 18. | … | Qc6 |
| 19. | Rb1† | |

Bravo! The Bishop is still working too hard. *19… Bxb1 20. Qxc6+−*. *19… Ka7 20. Bb5†*. Or best, *19… Ka8 20. Bb7†! Kb8 21. Qa8#*.

| 19. | … | Resigns. |

Decimals? Fractions? In chess? Mr. Viens makes things all add up.

### w: Edward Viens (UNR)
### b: Tom Tucker (Master)
King's Gambit Declined B07
## MENARD RIVER ROOKS VS. MADISON COUNTY (IL) CA
## MATCH 1989

| 1. | e4 | d6 |
|----|----|----|
| 2. | d4 | Nf6 |
| 3. | Nc3 | Nfd7 |

Not in the books. So what do you do? Think. Try to figure out the difference between book and non-book moves, and whether there's a message therein.

Some moves aren't in the books because they're too awful for words—or ECO symbols. 3... Nxe4 isn't in the books, and you won't find 3... Kd7 (until my friend NM Jack Young writes *his* book).

Other moves aren't that terrible, they just have a pretty obvious flaw or shortcoming. Thus here 3... e6 is certainly "playable," but it's not played. Too passive, too unassuming. It is clear that there are better moves

(3... g6; 3... c6), even if it is not clear which of these is best.

So how bad is 3... Nfd7? It's hard to quantify. A guess: if White was .1P better after 3. Nc3, he is probably .2- or .3P better now.

Why did Black play it? To support ...e7-e5. He makes a "strongpoint" of the e5-square with ...Nd7, ...Nc6, ...Be7-f6. That's a strategy common to several rather old-fashioned 1. e4 e5 opening variations. It is solid and defensive, but can be a bit like a coiled spring. The strongpoint pieces can turn out to be very effectively placed if the object of their attention is removed under the right circumstances. But White can usually control this and maintain a comfortable advantage.

But Black usually reaches such a "strongpoint" position in a more normal way: 1... e5, 2... Nc6, 3... d6, then perhaps ...g6 and ...Bg7 or ...Nge7-g6, ...Be7-f6. He develops his game a little more before he starts moving pieces a second time.

What difference does that make? If you move a piece for a second time on Move 6, you are "wasting" one sixth of your moves; if on Move 3, you waste one third!

Can White take advantage of this? Black is wasting time; White could try to underline this by developing *quickly* and with immediate point. Sharpest is 4. *Bc4!* If Black plays his intended 4... e5, 5. *Qf3* could be embarrassing. One natural defense, 5... *Qe7*, runs into 6. *Nd5*—there's no Knight on f6! If he puts one there with 5... *Nf6*, it looks as if Black has made three reasonable moves while White has made five—and it's White's move. But it's that or 5... *f6*, with a big White advantage in either case.

**4. f4**

This is fine. Also good would be 4. *Nf3* or 4. *Be3* or 4. *Be2*....

Normal straightforward development is good versus unusual moves, unless there's accompanying unusual danger. That's ob-

viously not the case here.

| 4. | ... | e5 |
| 5. | Nf3 | Nc6 |
| 6. | Bc4 | Be7 |

"If 6... Na5, I had planned 7. Bxf7† Kxf7 8. de5 *threatening* Qd5† *and* Ng5†."

—Viens

Pretty convincing. It would indeed be surprising if there were not a refutation of further neglect of development by Black.

| 7. | 0-0 | 0-0 |
| 8. | a3?! | |

So he can answer ...*Na5* with *Ba2.*

Not a terrible idea, but it is not a very efficient use of time. And I'm not sure it's all that important to keep the Bishop on that diagonal. If ...*Na5 Bd3* or *Be2*, White's Bishop seems better-placed than Black's Knight.

I'd prefer 8. *Be3*. After 8. *a3*, Black could take twice on d4, then hit the Queen with ...*Bf6*, then the Bishop with ...*Nb6*. White would still be better, but the exchanges and tempi would ease Black's congestion and help him develop.

But Black continues the strongpoint play.

| 8. | ... | Bf6?! |

**9. fe5**

Probably best, but 9. *Be3* is still okay. Then exchanges on d4 would land the Queen there, and it could not now be conveniently driven away. And otherwise, White could follow up with *Qd2* and *Rad1* or *Rf2, Raf1*. Development is rarely a bad idea!

| 9. | ... | de5 |
|----|-----|-----|
| 10. | d5 | Ne7 |
| 11. | Bg5?! | |

But this is more than "just" development. Look at the locked pawns. White should keep this Bishop. Why trade for that big pawn on f6? *11. Be3!, Qd2, Rad1....* White can smoothly mobilize all of his forces. How about Black? With more difficulty, certainly. Don't help him do it!

Possibly we have some wishful thinking by White here. *If 11... Bxg5 12. Nxg5 Ng6?* (or *12... h6? 13. Nxf7 Rxf7 14. d6) 13. Qh5 h6 14. Nxf7*, White wins. But Black can improve

*(12... Nf6)*, and, anyway, *11... Bxg5* isn't near forced.

But you can hallucinate into thinking it *almost* is! Exchange possibilities sometimes do that. Of all the things that can happen, isn't *...Bxg5* the most obvious? Sometimes, that can slip into "most likely."

But exchanges are just moves! After *5. Nf3 Nc6* the position has changed, and we have to deal with that. Likewise after *9. fe5 de5*. A capture is often more forcing, but is not necessarily so. The evaluation process is the same whether a swop is involved or not.

Helpful Hint Department: Note that when *you* take a piece, you usually bring an enemy piece forward, helping *him* develop. This doesn't mean it's always a bad idea! But it always needs thinking about.

| 11. | ... | Ng6 |
|-----|-----|-----|
| 12. | Bxf6 | Nxf6 |

*Look* at what happened in the last two moves! The dark-squared Bishops vanished, White made two moves with a piece that no longer exists, while the black Knights jumped from d7 and e7 to f6 and g6. Black could not have done much better had he been selecting moves for both sides.

| 13. | Qe1 | Qd6 |
|-----|-----|-----|

With a pretty obvious threat—check all checks, mind your unprotected pieces, don't stop when you spot ...Qc5xc4. There's another check, a loose b-pawn.

So what do we do? Examine the candidates:

• *14. Kh1* is simplest, may be best. It allows you to postpone a Bishop or pawn decision. Quick—where should the Bishop go?? Hard to be sure, but the King is going nowhere if not to h1.

• *14. Bb3* secures Bishop and b-pawn, but with the pawn on d5 the Bishop is not that well-placed here. Black could develop with ...Bd7, then consider his pawn breaks, ...c6 or ...f5, or look to maneuver. White's strongest plan is *Rc1, c4-c5*, but it also takes the most time. Black's position should be able to meet that, especially since *Ne2* and *c4* hang the Bishop to ...Qb6† and *Na4 Bd7; c4 Bxa4, Bxa4 Qc5†* bags

the c-pawn.

• Another idea is *Nh4*. It's okay, but again Black should be up to the task, probably either with ...Nf4 or ...Nh5-f4. But— remember?—it would not be good to bring White forward with *14... Nxh4 15. Qxh4*, when he's ready for a Rook lift to g3 or doubling on the f-file.

• *14. Bd3* looks better than *Bb3*. The b-pawn? A Wise Old Man at Boston's venerable Boylston Chess Club once said, "He who takes the b-pawn with his Queen in the early middlegame will sleep in the street." What he meant was *14. Bd3 Qb6† 15. Kh1 Qxb2? 16. Nh4*. With the Bishop (central-ized) on d3, it's a little easier to run up the c-pawn. And White can play *Ne2* without hanging e4.

• The move played.

**14.  b4**

I don't like it. I'm suspicious of all pawn moves. Call it a preju-dice.

What's wrong with *14. b4*? If you later regret *14. Kh1*, you can always ... play *Kg1*. There will never again be a white pawn on b2.

All pawn moves attack, "control" squares, but they also give up control of squares. c3 will never again have pawn protection. This is not something to give up lightly. We'll see why.

A second problem with *14. b4*, unlike, say, *Bd3* or *Kh1*, is that it gives Black something to play against. Let's jump ahead a bit, only noting that Black could play an immediate *14... a5*. Perhaps he didn't like *15. Nb5*, but after *15... Qb6† 16. Kh1 Bd7* White must fall back (*17. Qe2?! Bxb5 18. Bxb5 Nxe4!*).

**14. ...        Bd7**
**15. Bd3**

Anyway! White sees that if Black plays *...a5* his best response is *b5*, but that would lose the *B/c4* to *...Qc5†*.

Black does indeed now play *15... a5*. It's okay, or Black could try *...Nf4* or *...Nh5-f4* and keep *...a5* as an option. That's one point about *14. b4*: Black can (or not!) play against it at will. White will always have to be alert to the possibility, thus *15. Bd3*.

Second point: Remember the weakened c3-square? How to get at it? Open the c-file. *15... c6* sure suggests itself. White doesn't have a good way to hold d5: *16. Bc4? a5* (heh, heh, heh), and if *16. dc6* Black can recapture with Bishop or Queen (*16... Qxc6!? 17. Bb5? Qb6†*) with strong and obvious play—*...Rc8* and *...Rd8*, or *...Rfc8* and *...a5*.

Now put the pawn back on b2 and see how less effective *...c6* is.

In Sum: Push a Pawn, Burn a Bridge.

**15. ...        a5**
**16. b5**

Black's *15... a5* was not a bad idea either. Now I think he can still play *...c6* to good effect.

**16. ...        a4**

There goes another Bridge.

Perhaps Black feared *Na4, c4* (*...b6*), *Qc3*, and *c5*, but he could meet that with *...c6!?* or *...b6*, *...Bg4*, *...Nd7-c5*.

Or he might have played *16... a4* for positive reasons. He may have thought he could put enough pressure on b5 to prevent White from winning a4 or playing *c2-c4* effectively.

Or maybe it was a positional—eventual!—pawn sac. It will be decentralizing for White to go after a4, once it's gone a3 will be weak, and a White win because he won *that* pawn is a long way down the road. Black will get some compensation for his a-pawn; whether it's enough for dynamic equality—or more!—we'll have to try to figure out.

White now goes after a4 with all deliberate speed, while Black uses the holes *b4-b5* left behind to position his pieces.

| | | |
|---|---|---|
| 17. | Qd2 | Qc5† |
| 18. | Kh1 | b6 |
| 19. | Rfb1 | Ra5 |
| 20. | Rb4 | Rfa8 |
| 21. | Rab1 | Qe7 |

Covering e5 so he can move the N/g6, and getting out of the way of his Knights, which are heading for c5 and d6 and maybe points beyond.

White can't take a4 yet; a3 would go. So he decides to cover b5 with *c2-c4*. This is consistent with his plans and, I *suppose*, not that bad. But need I mention that the c-pawn gives up control of b3, and potential control of d4? Do you smell smoke?

| | | |
|---|---|---|
| 22. | Ne2 | Ne8 |
| 23. | c4 | Nd6 |
| 24. | Qc2 | Bg4 |

Primarily to clear d7 for the Knight. Yes, it is a "good" Bishop, but it is not necessarily a mistake to exchange it. A bad Bishop is usually a more important factor than a good Bishop. All of Black's pieces are pretty

"good," but White's Knights are significantly more useful than his Bishop. So right now one third of White's minor pieces are bad. After *25… Bxf3*, half will be bad.

| | | |
|---|---|---|
| 25. | Nc3 | Bxf3 |
| 26. | gf3 | Nf8 |
| 27. | Rxa4 | Nd7 |
| 28. | Rxa5 | Rxa5 |
| 29. | a4 | Nc5 |
| 30. | Ra1 | Qg5 |

Whether *16… a4* was sacrifice or miscalculation, Black has full compensation for his pawn.

An extra pawn is a Good Thing because it can help you control more squares than your opponent can, or because you can advance it to queen or use that threat to force the enemy back. White's extra pawn (on a4) is a decided underachiever.

Another factor in Black's favor is White's bad Bishop. All it can do is defend, and it's particularly impotent versus Black's Knights. Even if White could figure out how to swop the N/c3 for the N/c5, he could never lift the blockade (…*Nd6-b7-c5!?*). White should point out the window and, when Black turns to look, slide the Bishop to d2. *Then* he could win.

*And* Black's pieces are more active, having no passive defensive chores.

| | |
|---|---|
| 31. | Qe2 |

To stop *31... Qe3.* Now Black could try *...Kf8-g8-f8,* and I don't see a winning plan for White. Instead, Black shifts his Knights to apparently even stronger posts.

| 31. | ... | Nb3 |
| 32. | Rb1 | Nd4 |
| 33. | Qf2 | Qf4 |
| 34. | Kg2 | Nb7 |

*"Both of us were in time trouble here. If Black had moved 34... Qg5† I might have consented to draw by repetition."*

—Viens

That would be a logical conclusion to the game.

Now, since Black has let up on c4, White should try *Bc2-d1* as a more efficient setup, particularly in view of the next note.

| 35. | Rb2 | Nc5 |
| 36. | Bc2 | |

| 36. | ... | Ra8? |

*"Here I was very afraid of 36...*

Qc1 37. Ra2 Nd3 38. Bxd3 Qxc3 *where I'd have no better than 39. Bf1 conceding my a-pawn."*

—Viens

And then the Knight would be so much better than the Bishop that Black would have the advantage. Perhaps not enough to win, but plenty enough to decline a draw.

Indeed, the black pieces are *so* active that it would be surprising if there weren't something good here, especially since the N/c3 and R/b2 are both loose. Hmmm. Could there be something better than ...Qc1? Keres said, when you find a good move, don't play it—look for a better one. *36... Qc1* was *good,* but can we do it with tempo? *36... Qg5†* now is even better than two moves ago. If the King goes back, *37... Qc1†* wins Rook or Knight (if *38. Bd1*). And if *36... Qg5† 37. Qg3, ...Qd2†* wins.

So *36... Qg5† 37. Kh3* is forced. But *Kh3* does not inspire confidence. Black has lots of good ideas. *...Ra8-d8-d6-h6* and *...Nd7-f6-h5-f4* are both slow but strong. *Hmmm.* And Vien's second suggestion is now even better for the check: *37... Qc1! 38. Ra2 (38. Nd1 Nxa4* probably wins) *Nd3 39. Bxd3 Qxc3* and now, since the King isn't covering f3, White can't play *Bf1*. But it's very grim after *40. Be2 Qb3 41. Ra1 Qb2 42. Re1 Rxa4* (△ *...Ra2–+*).

Instead, alas, Black gets a bad idea. Time trouble is likely a factor.

**37. Ra2          h5**

This does not turn out to be much of a weapon, and eventually becomes a liability. Black's aggression is not justified once White has time to play *Bd1*, *Qe3*, and *Rg2*, when he has as much force as Black does on the Kingside.

**38. Bd1          h4**
**39. Qd2          Qf6**
**40. Qe3          g6**
**41. Kh1**

"*41. Kh3 is probably better. 41. Kh1 allowed 41... h3.*"

—Viens

Ironically, the King would now be safer on h3 than it would have been four moves ago, because the black h-pawn is a shield.

And, yes, *41... h3* is probably a good idea, to stop *Rg2*.

**41. ...          Kg7**
**42. Rg2          Rh8**
**43. Rg4**

With the idea *44. f4*. Black is in trouble anyway, but now blunders. Suddenly, White's terrible Bishop becomes the most effective piece on the board.

**43. ...          Rh5?**
**44. f4          ef4**
**45. Rxf4          Qe5**
**46. Bxh5          gh5**
**47. Rxh4**

It's all over. White finishes up very efficiently. He has played solid, practical chess throughout, with two Bishop exceptions. He should not have given up his good Bishop with Moves 11 and 12, and he should have been more efficient with the bad one on Move 35.

**47. ...          Nd7**
**48. Qg3†          Qxg3**
**49. hg3          Kg6**
**50. g4          hg4**
**51. Rxg4†          Kh5**
**52. Rg7          Ne5**
**53. c5          bc5**
**54. a5          Resigns**

Droll. The "decided underachiever" ends the game.

## PART IV — Endings

I love endings. Chess is about pieces and Pawns. The fewer there are, the more we can learn about them, the more their characteristic strengths and weaknesses become starkly apparent.

Word association: Ending—"Pure;" "Distillation;" "Essence."

If you have any doubt about what to study, study endgames. Openings teach you openings. Endings teach you chess.

I like all the games in this book but not all of them would appear in a more usual collection. This one would. It would grace *any* anthology. It was an honor to annotate it.

**w: Allan Savage (FM)**
**b: Stefan Djuric (GM)**
Ruy Lopez C68/6
CANADIAN OPEN 1983

**1. e4**

It is said that World Champion Emanuel Lasker played this move with a view to winning the ending.

**1. ... e5**
**2. Nf3 Nc6**
**3. Bb5 a6**
**4. Bxc6 dc6**

Here Lasker (most famously, but among others, of course) would play 5. d4 ed4 6. Qxd4 Qxd4 7. Nxd4. His classic point is that if you remove all the pieces save the Kings, the pawn ending is won for White. He can use his four pawns versus three on the Kingside to create a passed pawn, while Black's Queenside four are compromised—he can't force a passed pawn. If you have a training part-

ner, try playing this pawn ending out; it's very instructive.

But the won pawn ending does not mean the position after 7. Nxd4 is won. It's not that easy to trade all the pieces off, and the position is open enough for Black's two Bishops to compensate for the fractured pawn structure.

Note that White can't win a pawn with 5. Nxe5, since 5... Qd4 attacks both e4 and e5.

**5. 0-0**

But now 6. Nxe5 is a threat, since Black can't play 6... Qd4 7. Nf3 Qxe4? (8. Re1).

White doesn't expect that to happen, naturally. The point of 5. 0-0 is to delay a d-pawn decision, to see how Black covers e5, then to decide if *d2-d3* or *d2-d4* is best.

5... *f6* is perhaps now most common, usually answered by 6. *d4*. Other Black 5th moves are ...*Qf6*, ...*Ne7*, ...*Qe7*, ...*Bd6*, ...*Qd6*, some met by 6. *d3*, some 6. *d4*, some either, some by further delay....

**5.   ...        Be7**

Rare. The immediate point is that with the e-file blocked White can't win e5, since Black *can* play ...*Qd4xe4*.

Now White must decide how far to push his d-pawn.

**6.   d3!**

After 6. *d4 ed4* the black Bishop would have great scope on f6.

Now—need it be said?—White threatens 7. *Nxe5*.

**6.   ...        Bf6**

Let's compare this position with the "Lasker" position discussed after Black's 4th. White does not have as great a pawn-structure advantage. With pawns on d3 and e5, a winning ending is

even further away, and Black has more pawn influence in the center. On the other hand, with those two pawns on, the black Bishops have less scope, so each side's advantages are less pronounced.

The play there is more clearcut, more "open." Here we will have more subtle maneuvering as each player tries to create positions favoring his attributes. With smaller advantages, they must grind finer.

**7.   Be3        Ne7**

Many setups are reasonable. ECO gives only Georgadze–Novopasin 1975: 8. *h3 Ng6* 9. *Nc3 0-0* 10. *Qd2* (*10. d4!?*) *Re8* 11. *Ne2 Be6* 12. *Ng3 Qd7*, and now suggests *13. d4 ed4 14. Bxd4 Rad8 15. Rfd1±*.

White decides to leave his pawn on d3, at least for the moment, and probe Black's flawed Queenside.

**8.   Nbd2        Ng6**
**9.   Nc4        0-0**
**10.  a5        b6**

Otherwise White will play 11. *a5*, when *Nc4* and *Be3* will make it difficult for Black to ever advance his b-pawn. That will mean Space for White, perhaps for *Nf3-d2-b3-c5*, *Qd2-b4*, *Ra3-b3*, or some such setup. Black could survive that, but decides Life will be easier if his pawns are not fixed where they stand.

White can force in *a4-a5*, but not in quite so advantageous circumstances.

| 11. | b4 | Re8 |
|-----|-----|-----|
| 12. | a4 | b5 |
| 13. | Ncd2 | |

The difference? With the b-pawns advanced, White doesn't have that space advantage; he has fewer squares to play on. So what's his point? He has secured c5 as a base of operations. Indeed, in a sense he has been after that square since Move 4. That's when he caused Black's d-pawn to forsake c5 (among other things). Then *12. a4* took the b-pawn away from that square.

A small thing? Sure. White won't win the game just because he "won" c5. But in such a closed position, he's in the business of accumulating small advantages. Use of c5 is one. He'll use that to look for more, to probe Black's weak points—a6, c6, e5.

And what of Black? The (then) newly minted (1982) GM didn't come all the way from (then) Yugoslavia to roll over and die because FM Savage seized a square. He will cover his weak spots as efficiently as possible and look for play elsewhere, center or Kingside. And he will look for a chance to open the position (*…f5!?*) to enhance his two Bishops' prospects.

| 13. | ... | Be7 |
|-----|-----|-----|
| 14. | Rb1 | f6 |
| 15. | Qe1 | |

To cover b4 when he plays *Nb3*.

Black could—i.e., it's legal—now play *15… f5*, but after *16. ef5* both c5 and e4 would be safely available to White's pieces. Black doesn't want to surrender another square! He will play …g6, then …f5, to recapture with a pawn there. Meanwhile, he centralizes his Knight to e6, where it watches c5, d4, and f4, and he furthers his development.

In contrast to many games in this book, such slow maneuvering is possible because of the closed nature of the position.

| 15. | ... | Nf8 |
|-----|-----|-----|
| 16. | Nb3 | Bg4 |
| 17. | Nh4 | Ne6 |
| 18. | f3 | Bh5 |
| 19. | Nf5 | Bf8 |
| 20. | Qc3 | Bg6 |

Black is not worried about *21. Qxc6?! Bxb4*, "solving" his doubled pawn problem.

Now White avoids *21… Bxf5*. He does not fear the doubled pawns so much as he does not want to give up pawn control of d5. The black Queen could be happy there.

| 21. | Ng3 | Bf7 |
|-----|-----|-----|

**22.  Rbd1**

A natural move that is hard to fault, but *22. Ne2* might be just a little better. It supports both of White's potential pawn breaks, *f3-f4* and—especially—*d3-d4*.

*22. d4* immediately would gain White nothing. After pawns and Knights came off, Black could set up smoothly and actively with *....Bc4*, *...Qe7*, *...Rad8*, later perhaps *...Qf7* and *...Bd6-e5*, depending on White's moves.

But that variation looks better for White after *22. Ne2*. Then he can finish capturing on d4 with a Knight, when c6 would be under real, rather than apparent, pressure.

Not that White would *have* to follow *Ne2* with *d3-d4*. But the more seriously he can threaten it, the more seriously Black has to take it. That's important. It limits Black's possibilities. And vice versa—White

must either work to prevent *...f5* or be ready to react appropriately when it comes.

All this is very nerve-racking and time-consuming. In a way, sharp tactical positions may be easier to play. There, "all" you have to do is try to calculate; here, you must first decide if you need to.

Black's next is a fine dual-purpose move. By inducing *23. Nc5*, Black makes an immediate *d3-d4* less likely; that move would then cost White his Bishop for the black Knight. And *...Qd6* covers e5, making an eventual *...f5* possible.

**22.  ...          Qd6**
**23.  Nc5          g6**
**24.  Ne2          Bg7**

With Black poised for *...f5*, White must have now been tempted by a preemptive *25. d4*. But after *25... f5*—anyway!—the opening of the position favors Black's two Bishops. One example: *26. ef5 gf5 27. de5 Qxe5 28. Qxe5 Bxe5*, when *29... Nxc5 30. Bxc5 Bxh2†* (or *30... Bc4!*) is in the air.

Many other variations are possible, which the Reader is invited to explore. The two Bishops should be adequate, not so much to defend Black weaknesses as to seek out positive counter-chances.

**25. Kh1          f5**

This is an ideal pawn formation for Black. White won't take—*26. ef5? gf5* reduces his influence in the center and allows Black to threaten to push either e- or f-pawns. And as it stands, Black retains the option of *...f4* or, less likely, *...fe4*.

White doesn't like this. He wants Black to make a decision. So he removes his Queen from the gaze of the black Bishop, and so introduces the possibility of *27. f4*.

**26. Qd2          f4**

This *is* good for Black, but not as good as maintaining the pawns abreast, if he but could. Now White "knows where he lives," and, while *...g5-g4-g3* is plenty dangerous, at least White knows *that's* what he has to worry about. I think he should now play *27. Bg1*, as he must later.

**27. Bf2          g5**
**28. Nb7          Qd7**
**29. Qc3          g4**
**30. d4**

Doubly thematic—White meets a wing attack with action in the center and strikes at the base of Black's pawn chain.

Is White opening the game for Black's two Bishops, as we earlier feared? To a degree, but less so. The advanced black pawns, while more threatening, are also more vulnerable. And the white Knights are better-placed now. If Black takes, he will have to either see Bishops exchanged on d4 or have c6 come under real pressure.

We do the best we can with general principles, but tactics have the final say.

Both players are likely getting short of time.

*"Time controls at move 40, 60. Both involved massive mutual time-trouble."*

—Savage

**30. ...          g3**
**31. Bg1**

A similar g-pawn advance occurs in many King's Indian Defense variations, and—in general—it is dangerous for White to take the pawn on g3. Here, it is impossible. If White's Knight or Bishop takes on g3, then d4 will lack adequate protection. And if White plays *31. de5?*, he will have two pieces hanging after *31... Qc8-+*.

Now Black's *31... Rab8* looks neither useful nor necessary. I like *31... Qe7*, heading for h4 posthaste.

**31. ...          Rab8**
**32. de5          Qe7**
**33. Qxc6**

White grabs a pawn, but also

increases his activity. He wants to draw Black away from the Kingside. Both players doubtless low on time.

| 33. | ... | Bxe5 |
| 34. | c3 | Qh4 |
| 35. | Nc5 | Nxc5 |

Perhaps 35... Ng5!? △ ...Bc4, ...Rbd8.

| 36. | Qxc5 | Bd6 |
| 37. | Qc6 | Re5 |

Black's threat is ...Rh5, ...Be6-h3xg2†, ...Qh3, ...g2. If White takes the Bishop on h3, ...Qxh3 and ...g2.

Whether or not White sees that, he knows instinctively that he must interrupt the flow toward h1.

With his flag rising ...

| 38. | Rxd6! | cd6 |
| 39. | Qxd6 | Rbe8 |
| 40. | Rd1 | |

| 40. | ... | Bb3?! |

*"I made the first time control with 30 seconds left; he had 10 seconds! Much better was 40... Bc4! I spent 25*

*minutes on my 41. h3!!, the best move of the game. After Move 42, taking the 2nd exchange, the position is quite unique and very pretty! Dead equal (well, not quite dead)."*

—*Savage*

Indeed, if 40... Bc4 White could not play the natural 41. Nd4 because his Bishop would have no squares after 41... gh2 (42. Bxh2? Rh5). And 40... Bc4 41. Rd2 is out because of 41... gh2 42. Bd4 Qe1†. So White would have to answer 40... Bc4 with the passive 41. Nc1?! or the defensive 41. Qd2. And the latter move would allow Black to capture the Knight instead of the Rook. Yes—"allow"! In those 25 minutes, White discovered that his Knight is more valuable than his Rook.

That's what's so good about 41. h3. White realized he can create a position that is not Rook-Friendly. The logistics are such that it would be easier to sac a Bishop or a Knight than a Rook on h3. But by the time Black worked his Bishop around to that diagonal, White could easily hold with Bd4 and Ng1.

Besides, Black's Mother taught him that to be up an exchange is a Good Thing; to be up two of 'em must be twice as good....

| 41. | h3!! | R5e6 |
|-----|------|------|
| 42. | Qd2 | Bxd1 |
| 43. | Qxd1 =! | Qf6 |
| 44. | Bd4 | Qf7 |
| 45. | Qd2 | Rf8 |
| 46. | Bc5 | Ree8! |

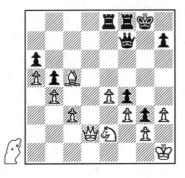

*"I liked his trapping of his own Rook on Move 46; a Rook that is clearly inferior to the Bishop! I never considered taking it."*

*—Savage*

Indeed, after *47. Bxf8? Rxf8* Black could try to penetrate on the d- or c-files, and offer to trade f4 for c3—or for the chance to get the Rook to d1 (ouch).

| 47. | Kg1! | Qb3 |
|-----|------|------|
| 48. | Kf1 | |

Of course not *48. Nxf4? Qb1†.*

| 48. | ... | Rf7 |
|-----|------|------|
| 49. | Ke1 | h5 |
| 50. | Bd4 | h4 |

Black has no good winning try. The only way a Rook can get in is via c3 or d4, and White controls them adequately. This is a great example of the *relative* value of the pieces — "It all depends on the position." Take the a-pawns off, and Black could win.

So why is he playing? There's that time control at Move 60....

| 51. | Bc5 | Kh7 |
|-----|------|------|
| 52. | Bd4 | Rd8 |

Beware Yugoslavs bearing gifts. He would *love* for White to grab f4. That would take the Knight away from d4—the most important square on this board. *53. Nxf4? Rxd4! 54. cd4 Qb1† 55. Ke2 Rc7,* and we see a Rook that *amounts* to a Rook.

| 53. | Qc1 | Rd6 |
|-----|------|------|
| 54. | Qd2 | Rdd7 |
| 55. | Qc1 | Rc7 |
| 56. | Qd2 | Rcd7 |
| 57. | Qc1 | Rc7 |

As the flags rise again …

| 58. | Qd2 | Rc4 |
|-----|------|------|
| 59. | Qc1 | Rd7 |

*Seconds left. The c-pawn is pinned. He can play 60... Rdxd4 61. Nxd4 Qxc3†. Maybe 60. Qd2!?? No—same line. A Rook gets in. The clock....*

| 60. | Qxf4 | Qb1† |
|-----|------|------|

*"Black made the time control with 2 seconds to spare! Then we adjourned overnight. Analysis showed that any winning attempts by either side only lead to inferior positions."*

*—Savage*

The point of 60. *Qxf4* is that if Black doesn't have a mate, White will have a perpetual. Black doesn't have a mate. The amazing balance continues.

| 61. | Kd2 | Rcxd4† |
| 62. | Nxd4 | Rxd4† |
| 63. | cd4 | Qb2† |
| 64. | Kd1 | Qxg2 |
| 65. | Qxh4† | |

Amazing. Black was up two exchanges; suddenly he's down three pawns. But the one on g3 is worth four of White's. It's all relative.

| 65. | ... | Kg8 |
| 66. | Qd8† | Kh7 |
| 67. | Qd7† | Kh8 |
| | **Drawn** | |

*"One of the best games I ever played."*

—*Savage*

A sporting success forsure by Mr. Colby, then a nod to The Real World.

**w: Daniel Lee (2353)**
**b: Kenneth Colby (1832)**

Sicilian Defense B35(10)

### Santa Monica Bay Area Chess Club Rating Tnmt., 8/9/93

| | | |
|---|---|---|
| 1. | e4 | c5 |
| 2. | Nf3 | Nc6 |
| 3. | d4 | cd4 |
| 4. | Nxd4 | g6 |
| 5. | Nc3 | Nf6 |
| 6. | Be3 | Bg7 |
| 7. | Bc4 | Qa5 |

*Be there dragons??*

Not here, not today. Without ...d6, Black's pawns do not bear their fanciful resemblance to a Dragon. And not only does the beast we have here not look like a Dragon, it doesn't behave like one.

If this were a *real* Dragon, the Queen would be on d8 and the pawn on d6, White would play 8. *Qd2*, Black, ...0–0, and if White decided on 0–0–0, *then* Black might play ...*Qa5*.

So what's with this early ...*Qa5*?

First, while ...*Qa5* is in general a plausible move, it has more point versus 0–0–0. Thus here, White's best is thought to be 8. 0–0, fleeing the Queen and continuing often with *Nb3* and/or *f4*, when ...*Qa5* does not turn out to be particularly useful to Black.

Second, there *is* a point to ...*Qa5* that White can't ignore.

It pins the Knight, and so threatens 8... Nxe4. (Thus 8. 0-0!?). White can't blithely make normal "Dragon" moves and hope for 8... d6 and 9... 0-0. For example, 8. Qd2? is known to be bad — it runs into 8... Nxe4! If 9. Nxe4, Black takes the Queen, then the Knight on d4, coming out a safe pawn ahead. So White might try 9. Nxc6, moving the d4 target, taking a piece, and hitting Black's Queen. Looks *good* — but loses to 9... Qxc3!

**8. f3?**

Surely *this* secures e4. Alas, no. 8. 0-0!

| 8. | ... | Qb4 |
| 9. | Bb3 | Nxe4! |

Because if White takes the Knight, he drops the one on d4. Matulovic–Toran 1967 is one example — 10. fe4 Bxd4 11. Bxd4 Qxd4 12. Qf3 e6 13. a4 a6 14. h4 h5 15. Rd1 Qe5∓.

So he tries ...

| 10. | Nxc6 | Bxc3† |
| 11. | bc3 | Qxc3† |
| 12. | Ke2 | dc6 |

The only move. It frees the Bishop so to answer 13. fe4? with ...Bg4†.

Now ECO shows Black winning after 13. Qg1 Nf6 14. Bd4 Qb4 15. Qe3 0-0 16. Radl b6.

But why set up Bd4 with 13. Qg1? Why not play it at once?!

**13. Bd4**

Because there's no big threat! See the Knight fork on c3? "All" Black must do is safeguard his Rook. Best may be 13... 0-0, but Black prefers a forcing move.

| 13. | ... | e5 |
| 14. | Bxc3 | Nxc3† |
| 15. | Kf2 | Nxd1† |
| 16. | Raxd1 | Ke7 |

As good as Black deserves to feel, by that amount he should resist complacency. There's a *lot* of work left.

I liked 13... 0-0 to avoid making the e-pawn the target it is now. I like 16... 0-0 to shelter the King — you *know* Rhe1 is coming. 16... 0-0 17. Rhe1 Re8 18. f4 Bg4 followed perhaps by 19... e4 looks better than the game.

| 17. | Rhe1 | f6 |
| 18. | f4 | Bg4 |
| 19. | Rd3 | Rad8 |
| 20. | Rde3 | Rhf8 |

He must return one pawn, and gets as much activity as he can for it.

| 21. | fe5 | fe5† |
| 22. | Kg3 | Bf5 |
| 23. | Rxe5† | Kf6 |
| 24. | h3 | h5 |

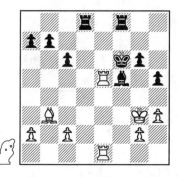

A pawn-plus isn't always enough to win. You want to gather as many additional trumps as you can. *24… h5* may become necessary; I don't think it is now. Better seems *24… Rd7 △ …Rfd8* and some penetration via d4 or d2. An immediate *24… Rd2* may not be good enough because White's *25. Re7* causes a waste of time — *25… Rd7*, when after *26. Rxd7 Bxd7 27. Rf1† Ke7 28. Rxf8 Kxf8 29. Kf4 h6 30. Ke5 Ke7* White's King position may be worth a pawn.

**25. R1e2       Rd6**

Cautious. Why not *25… Rd4?* We all learn the relative piece values — 1, 3, 3, 5, 9 — remember the numbers and forget the "relative." But *you* can adjust those, move by move. An active piece is worth more than a passive one. And while the in-

crease in a piece's stock is usually temporary, it can last long enough to … decide the game!

**26. Kf3       h4**

Surely best. Given the Bishops, it's good in general to get black pawns onto dark squares. And White was threatening to gain valuable space with *27. g4 hg4† 28. hg4 Bd7 29. g5†.*

**27. Ra5       a6**
**28. Ra4?!      g5**
**29. Kf2**

Unless there's a threat I don't see, it would be better to hurry the Rook back — *Ra5-e5.*

**29. …          Rfd8**
**30. Ra5       Rd2**

Not bad. Going for exchanges seems right … but you can't count on a pawn-plus being sufficient. Better to not count pawns — or to not *only* count pawns. Black has other advantages to utilize — better *effective* activity (White can't penetrate as quickly), better Bishop (especially with the weak white pawns on h3 and g2), more space, and a safer King.

Two ideas — *30… Rd4-f4†* and, depending on the response, *…Rd1* or *…g4.*

Even better — *30… g4!* at once. After *31. hg4 Bxg4* and White moves his Rook, *then 32… Rd2†* looks decisive. Black will target both g2 and the white

King.

Even in the game, the eventual ...g4 idea looks good. I'm not sure what White can play. *31. Ke1 Rd1† sure* doesn't help. And *31. Rae5 g4 32. hg4 Bxg4* is nothing but trouble.

Alas, the Real World often intrudes. Mr. Colby —

*It is 11 o'clock at night, we have been playing for three and a half hours, he has five minutes to make ten moves, I am giving away 40 years in age and I want to go home — so I offer a draw which he readily accepts because it is probably a win for Black by slowly picking off the pawns.*

A sporting, if not artistic, success. May we all do as well when out-rated by 521 points.

A second game from a gracious loser brings to mind a flaw in the scoring system. Sure Black won, but too much happened to call it all or nothing, 0—1. 40-60 seems about right.

### w: James Tanaka (1804)
### b: Alex Yarmulnik (1991)
Bird's Opening A03/1
## Mid-America Class Tnmt. 1993

| | | |
|---|---|---|
| 1. | f4 | d5 |
| 2. | Nf3 | Nc6 |
| 3. | e3 | Nf6 |
| 4. | b3 | a6?! |

Choosing Knight squares was easy; now Black is deciding where to put his Bishops. No doubt he would've answered 4. Bb5 with 4... Bd7. But now he wants the Bishop more actively posted on f5. But he fears Bb5. He should not. 4... Bf5 5. Bb5 a6 (5... e6? 6. Ne5 Qd6 7. Ba3) 6. Bxc6 bc6 is not bad for Black. The doubled pawns are not that weak, particularly since they are somewhat mobile and thus might be dissolved.

Another way to meet Black's concern is to delay developing the B/c8 until White moves the B/f1. Play might go 4... g6 5. Bb2 Bg7 6. Nc3 0-0, when White is due to move his Bishop.

The value of 4... a6 is not worth the waste of time.

| | | |
|---|---|---|
| 5. | Bb2 | Bf5 |
| 6. | a3?! | |

The value of 6. a3 is not worth the waste of time.

White fears ...Nb4, but there are more useful and efficient ways to deal with the attack on c2. Thus, after 6. Be2 Nb4? White does well with either 7. d3 or 7. Nd4. Then he may play 8. a3 if he wishes. But even in that case, it could be a waste of time if Black's Knight has nothing better to do than return to c6 anyway.

| | | |
|---|---|---|
| 6. | ... | Ne4?! |

White's reply (7. d3) is so easy to anticipate that Black

must *want* to relocate his Knight to d6. It's not a bad square, but not worth two moves to get there. Better would be 6... e6, 7... Be7, 8... 0-0.

And indeed, after 7. d3 Black's best move may be 7... Nf6! (I thought this even before I saw that the Knight visits b5, a7, c8 ...).

**7. d3          Nd6**

**8. Ne5**

Fine; also good are *8. Nbd2* and *8. Be2*.

Now if Black allows *Nxc6* his doubled pawns would not be a problem, but the open diagonal from b2 would make Kingside development difficult. Maybe *...f6, ...Nf7, ...e5!?*

| | | |
|---|---|---|
| 8. | ... | Nxe5 |
| 9. | fe5 | Nb5 |

*9... Nc8!?*

| | | |
|---|---|---|
| 10. | a4 | Na7 |
| 11. | Be2 | e6 |
| 12. | 0-0 | Qg5? |

Black should be suspicious of this, even without calculation.

He is behind in development, and White's weaknesses are not *that* weak.

**13. Bc1**

White's reply is fine. Also good would be *13. Rf3*, when if *13... Bg4 14. Rg3 Bxe2 15. Qxe2* he would be even further ahead in development.

Perhaps Black planned now *13... Bh3* and only now sees that it doesn't work. It shouldn't. He's outnumbered. *14. Rf2 (or 14. Bf3) Qxe5 15. d4 Qg5 16. e4 Qg6 17. ed5 ed5 18. Bh5* and captures on f7 and h3.

| | | |
|---|---|---|
| 13. | ... | Qd8 |
| 14. | Bg4 | Bg6 |
| 15. | d4 | |

Okay. Also good is development—*Nd2-f3* or *Nc3*.

Now Black should play *15... Be7* or *15... Nc8*. I don't see the point of the move he plays; perhaps he is thinking of *...0-0-0* and White's next changes his mind. In general, lining up the Queen vis-a-vis a white piece is not a good idea unless there's a compelling reason to do so.

| | | |
|---|---|---|
| 15. | ... | Qd7 |
| 16. | c4 | c6 |
| 17. | Nc3 | Bb4?! |
| 18. | Bd2 | Qe7 |
| 19. | c5 | |

Unnecessary, since the option to do this will remain. Black is unlikely to play *...dc4*, since it would only increase White's control of the center.

There is a tactical point to 19. c5, a Cheapo. See it?

White threatens to win a pawn with 20. Nxd5. That is not a good reason to play 19. c5.

**19. ... Bxc3**
**20. Bxc3**

Here, both players made small blunders. White offered a draw. Black declined.

**20. ... 0-0**

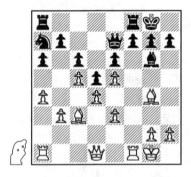

**21. Qd2**

Not a mistake, but not too constructive. What's the idea? We've just had a couple of "static," long-term events, locking the pawns (c5) and exchanging pieces (...Bxc3). A good time to reevaluate, decide on a plan, or at least on a piece setup.

The Plan—Kingside or Queenside?

Let's look at the Queenside. The obvious line-opener is b4-b5. With the Knight on a7, White will have to cover b5 with

Be2. How will Black react? It is (almost always) too much to hope for passive defense, especially when the opponent has just declined a draw! It's a good guess he'll meet Be2 with Kingside activity. A good guess is ...Be4, ...Qg5, ...f6. White can easily defend e3 and g2, but the f-file will open, two, likely four, Rooks will come off, and even granted that White neutralizes things there, what will happen on the Queenside? After b4-b5 Black can take with the a-pawn, then with the Knight. White will have to play BxN/b5 to make progress, but then we will probably have Queens and opposite-colored Bishops. Hard to see either side winning. Thus though the Queenside pawn structure calls for b4-b5, other factors argue against it.

Kingside? White is blessed. Action on that wing is also justified by the pawn structure—there's the half-open file and the cramping pawn on e5. Another factor in White's Kingside favor is on a7!

But how to proceed? How to set up? Sometimes, if you do the hard stuff first, the easy stuff takes care of itself. Which white piece will be the hardest to activate? Clearly, the Bishop on c3. How can we get it into play?

What *square* would we like it on? Doesn't h4 look good? How can we get it there? *Be1-g3, Qe1, Bh4* is a bit time-consuming, and the Queen is not all that well-placed on e1. How else? *Rf3-h3, Be1-h4* is better, but where do the Queen and Queen's Rook go? Rooks doubled on the f-file seems right. So how should the Queen cover h4? Ah! *Qf3-h3, Be1-h4, Rf4, Raf1*. Wouldn't *that* be a great setup? Especially so since *Qh3, Bh4* rules out an early *...f7-f6*.

I'd go for it. Black won't allow it. Play might go *21. Qf3 f6!? 22. ef6 Rxf6 23. Qh3 Bf5!? 24. Bxf5 Rxf5 25. Rxf5 ef5 26. Rf1 △ Rf3* (if *...Re8), Be1-h4* or *-g3-f4-e5-d6* as appropriate. White has a nice advantage: *three* active pieces, with chances to sift in on the dark squares (especially if *...g6)*. Meanwhile, Black will have a terrible time getting his Knight into play—*...Nc8-e7-g8-f6-e4*. He should live so long.

Moral: Don't look for a good move; look for a good *plan*.

| 21. | ... | Qg5 |
| 22. | Bh3 | |

More passive than necessary. Better would be *22. Bf3* or *22. Rf4* or *22. Qe2*. Now the black Bishop becomes powerfully posted.

| 22. | ... | Be4 |
| 23. | Ba5 | Qe7 |

Stopping *Bc7-d6*.

| 24. | Qe2 | Nc8 |
| 25. | Rf2 | |

Okay if he's planning *Raf1* or *g3, Bf1*.

Otherwise, he should go directly for his now-intended *Ra2-b2, Be1, b4-b5*. Queenside play is now indicated, because the Knight has given up b5 and White has given up Kingside ideas.

| 25. | ... | Qd7 |
| 26. | Ra2 | Ne7 |
| 27. | Rb2 | Rac8 |

Unnecessary. Not *bad*, but if White plays *b4-b5*, after *...ab5* this Rook looks better on a8.

**28. Rf4?!**

*"Mindless wandering."*

—Tanaka

| 28. | ... | Nf5 |

**29. g4**

Think before you kick. What will be accomplished? Is it important to kick *now*? Where will the

Knight go? To a safe square? To a better square? *29... Nh4* is an obvious possibility. Remember *h4?!* Why not *29. Be1!?* Whatever else, it gets this problem piece into the game. If Black covers h4 with *29... Qe7*, the black Queen will have left control of b5, making *b4-b5* easier. Or, if he must, White *can* kick, *30. g4*, then control the Knight after *30... Nh4* with *Bg3* and *Qe1*, perhaps with the idea *(...Ng6) Rf1, Bg2, h4-h5*.

The Point is that a move, especially a committing move like *g2-g4*, should be part of an overall scheme. As I used to shout as a tennis coach, "Have an idea out there."

**29. ...         Nh4**
**30. Qf2?**

*30. Be1!?* White's move is particularly questionable since Black's reply is so easy to predict.

**30. ...         Ng6**
**31. Rxe4**

Clearly best. Two Bishops can often do well versus Rook-and-Knight, harassing, controlling, restraining, avoiding exchanges. But if White had swopped Rook for Knight, the B/e4 and B/h3 would neutralize each other, and it would be "purely" B/a5-versus-Rook.

And from a purely practical point of view, White should now be able to pick up the pawn on e4.

**31. ...         de4**
**32. Qg2**

Not best. It is suspect on appearance alone—why immobilize your own Bishop, even briefly?

And the "analysis" is easy. How many times can Black defend e4? One time, for all practical purposes. Can we attack it twice? Sure. *Qc2* and *Bg2*. So play one of those *(32. Bg2!?)*, and if *32... Qd5*, play the other.

Occam's Razor works on a chessboard as well as in Science and Philosophy. There's truth in simplicity.

**32. ...         Qd5**
**33. g5**

Unpuckered, White must go through contortions to achieve the harmony he could've had with *Qc2* and *Bg2*. We leave him pondering The Simple Life, and turn to Black.

Time for *him* to get an idea, come up with a plan. He has just "won" an exchange. How should he use that advantage? According to its nature! Black has *Rooks*. How to use Rooks? On open lines. How can Black open a good line for a Rook? *33... f5!* White will surely take; otherwise, Black can simply hold e4 or, better, play *...f4!?*

After *34. gf6 gf6* White will likely take again, else *35... f5* or *35... fe5*. So *35. ef6*. Now Black has the happy choice of ...*Rxf6*, ...*Rcf8* or ...*Rxf6*, ...*Kh8*, ...*Rg8* or immediately ...*Kh8*, ...*Rg8*. And *then* see what a threat ...*Nh4-f3†* is!

The overall Point is: When pieces are functioning at their best, Rooks beat Bishops. So give your Rooks the best working conditions you can.

What Black plays is not so bad, but his Rooks are worth three times his Knight. Use 'em! Now.

**33.    ...        Nh4**

The problem is that White could now organize a semblance of a defense with *34. Qe2 △ Be1-g3*. Black would still be winning, but not so easily.

But White is looking only at e4 ...

| 34. | Qg4 | Nf3† |
| 35. | Kh1 | Kh8 |
| 36. | Bf1 | f5 |
| 37. | gf6 | gf6 |

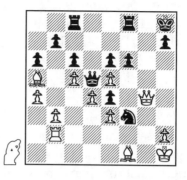

**38.    Bc4?**

Should lose at once. White has to play *38. Rg2* or *38. Bg2*, either of which loses more slowly.

Because now Black can play *38... Rg8!* (Tanaka). White can't move his Queen because of mate in one. And *39. Bxd5 Rxg4* either mates or wins the Bishop on d5. And *39. Qxg8† Rxg8 40. Rb1 Qd7* is equally resignable.

| 38. | ... | f5? |
| 39. | Bxd5 | fg4 |
| 40. | Bxe6 | Rce8 |
| 41. | Bc4 | |

A better try might be *41. Bxg4*. After *41... Rg8 42. Bxf3 ef3 43. Rf2 Ref8* Black should win, but there's a lot of work to do. Depending on White, Black may try in some combination ...*h5*, ...*Rg4*, ...*h4*, ...*h3*, ...*Rg2*, or if *h2-h3*, ...*Rg3*, meeting *Kh2* with ...*h4* or ...*Rfg8!*—or both, △ ...*Rg2* or ...*Rg1-b1* and ...*Rgg1*. It would be interesting, but Black should win.

Also good after *41. Bxg4* is *41... Ne1* (threatening mate!) *42. Bxe1 Rf1†* or *42. Be2 Nf3!* △ *43. Bxf3 Rxf3*.

**41.     ...          Re7**
**42.     Rf2**

Perhaps *42. b4!?, 43. b5*. It's hard to say where the Rook belongs until Black tries something. As it happens, he's still after mate on g1. Another idea is *...h5, ...h4, ...g3*, in part to make luft for Black's King! White might well try *42. Bc3!?* If Black proceeds as in the game, he runs into *42... Rg7?!* (*42... h5!*) *43. e6 g3? 44. d5*.

**42.     ...          Rg7**
**43.     e6           g3**
**44.     Rg2**

*44. hg3 Rxg3* threatens both *45... Rg1#* and, if *45. Rg2, ...Rh3†*.

*42. Rf2* was clearly a waste of time.

**44.     ...          gh2**
**45.     Rxg7         Kxg7**
**46.     e7**

Now *46. Bc3!?* (△ *d5†*) is a bit transparent. After *46... Kh6, 47... Rg8* is threatened, and the pawn is lost after *47. e7 Re8*.

**46.     ...          Re8**
**47.     Bd8          Kf6**

Safer and Surer and Easier on my Blood Pressure is *47... Ng5-f7xd8*.

Now I'm not even sure if

Black is winning!

Do you see White's move?

The key is the passed pawn. The key to *that* is the blockader, and we get at him via the light squares. *48. d5!* is *very* strong.

The first thing to note is that Black can't mate in two—*48... Rg8 49. e8=Q check*.

And if *48... cd5 49. Bxd5*, White has the b-pawn and e-pawn under fire, and Black can't play *49... Ke5* (△ *50. Bxb7? Rg8–+*) because of *50. Bf7*.

Black's only move is *48... Ne5*. Now *49. dc6* (*49. d6? Nxc4 50. d7 Rxe7*) *Nxc6 50. Bd5* could well draw. White threatens *Bxe4* and *b4* (*Nxb4*), *Bxb7*. If Black plays *50... Nxd8 51. ed8=Q† Rxd8 52. Bxe4* or *52. Bxb7!?*, White should be able to draw.

**48.     b4?          Nh4**
**49.     b5           ab5**
**50.     ab5          Nf5**
**51.     b6           Nxe3?**

Missing White's point. He should play *51... Nxe7 52. Bxe7*

*Rxe7* 53. d5 (again!) cd5 54. Bxd5 Ke5 55. Bc4 Rd7!, when Black wins by playing the Rook to c1 or c2.

**52. Ba6!**

Winning. Black should have asked himself why White played 51. b6. Now he knows.

**52. ... Nd5**
**53. Bxb7 Nxe7?!**

This gives White time to bag c6. Passed pawns should be pushed! More testing is *53... e3!?*, forcing *54. Ba6. Now 54... Nxe7 55. Bxe7† Rxe7* forces White to (again!) find *56. d5!* (*56. b7? Rxb7; 56. Be2? Ke6) cd5 57. c6*, and White will queen.

The key to both sides' best play (*53... e3!?; 56. d5!*) is the Great Power of the Passed Pawn. Also, note how vital each tempo can be in an ending. Every position must be analyzed precisely, of course, but your first try should be to forget material and rush ahead as fast as possible. If it doesn't work, then look for a more subtle approach. Thus here, White's best play is almost brutal in its single-minded push forward.

**54. Bxe7† Rxe7**
**55. Bxc6 e3**
**56. Bf3 Ke6**

If *56... e2 57. Bxe2 Rxe2, 58. c6* wins.

Now, after *56... Ke6,*

White's simplest win probably starts *57. Kxh2*, but to be consistent I suggest *57. d5†! Kd7 58. Bg4† Kd8 59. c6 e2 60. c7† Rxc7 61. bc7† Kxc7 62. Bxe2 Kd6 63. Bf3+−.*

But alas. After a wonderful struggle, White relaxes.

**57. b7? Rxb7**

*"Whoops! I forgot about the bugger on e3."*

—*Tanaka*

**58. d5†**

Sigh. About the only time it doesn't win.

**58. ... Ke5?!**

Or does it? This is playing with fire. Safe and Sure is *58... Ke7 59. d6† Kd8 60. Kxh2* (*60. Bxb7* would work if Black didn't queen with check) *e2! 61. Bxe2 Rb2.*

White is probably discouraged here. Understandably so. But if you play this game (and live this life), these things will happen. You will blunder. But White has already *paid* for *57. b7.* Don't pay for it again. Put it behind you. Relax. Smile. Use all the time you can afford to, and look at this position afresh. Deep-breathe now.

How to push those pawns? A Hint: We all know the advice against putting pawns on the same-colored squares as your Bishop. *Even now* it holds! And it *often* bears remembering when a Bishop helps advance two pawns. Why? Same reason as always: to control as many squares as possible.

Thus *59. d6!* The threat is *Kxh2, Kg3, Bxb7.* If Black again tries *59... Rb1† 60. Kxh2 e2 61. Bxe2 Rb2,* then *62. d7!* wins: *62... Rxe2† 63. Kg3 Rd2 64. c6.*

Then there's *59. d6 Rd7 60. Kxh2* (*60. c6? Rxd6 61. c7 e2! 62. Bxe2 Rc6–+*) *Kd4 61. c6 Rxd6 62. c7 e2 63. c8=Q e1=Q 64. Qg4†,* and I'd bet on a perpetual.

If Black heads for d2, we have *59. d6 Rb2 60. d7 Rd2 61. c6+–*.

Meanwhile, Black's clock is ticking ...

Okay, okay, Black *can* still win. But you see how he could go wrong. And after 59 moves he could be a little punchy. *And* he just played *...Ke6-e5.* It might be psychologically difficult to "find" *59... Ke5-e6! 60. Kxh2 Rb2† 61.*

*Kg3 Kd7! 62. Bg4† Kc6 63. d7 Kc7–+.* And it even stretches my point but I think the game is even easier for Black than *59. d6 Kf4 60. Be2 Kg3.*

Point is: Even if you're lost— or especially then!—work hard, make it tough on him. You'll save games.

**59. c6?!          Rb1†**
**60. Kxh2       Kd6**
Note the Bad Bishop.
**61. Kg3**

**61. ...          Rb2**
It would be clearer to get behind the pawn and push: *61... Rb8 62. Kg2 Re8 63. Kf1 Re5,* and Black will work the h-pawn down.

**62. Bg4          Rb4**
*62... Rb8!?* and *62... Rf2* both look better.

Now *63. Be6* loses to *63... Re4 64. Kf3 e2,* but White should simply go back to f3 and make Black find *...Rb8* or another winning idea. Instead, he makes it easy. See note to Black's 58th!

| 63. | Bh3? | Re4 |
|-----|------|-----|
| 64. | Bf5 | e2 |
| 65. | Bxe4 | e1=Q† |
| 66. | Kf4 | h5 |
| 67. | Bf3 | Qe5# |

An absorbing struggle.

A Lemansky Lesson about more than chess.

**w: David J. Hanson (1900)**
**b: Steve Lamansky (1805)**
Dutch Defense A88/11(55)
### AMES CHESS FESTIVAL 10/16/93

**1. d4      g6**

Black signals his willingness to play a Pirc or Modern after 2. *e4*. If he wants to assure a Dutch, he must play *1... f5*; but in that case he must be prepared to meet the Staunton Gambit, *2. e4*.

**2. c4      Bg7**
**3. Nc3      f5**

This move with ...*g6* defines the Leningrad Dutch, or, for the geopolitically up-to-date, the St. Petersburg Dutch. It is dynamic and double-edged, leading to unbalanced positions in which Black strives for the initiative rather than for cold equality. He pays for this with certain positional liabilities — often a weak d-pawn, weak e6- and f7-squares, and less central space. It is similar to the Sicilian, both in spirit

and superficial pawn definers — *1. e4 c5; 1. d4 f5*.

**4. g3      Nf6**
**5. Bg2      d6**
**6. Nf3      0-0**
**7. 0-0      c6**

This and *7... Nc6* were long the most common moves here. Recently, *7... Qe8* has become popular. It is very much in the flexible spirit of the Leningrad Dutch; depending on circumstances, the Queen can support ...*e7-e5* or ...*c6* and ...*b5*, or go to the Kingside after ...*h6* and ...*g5*.

**8. d5**

White plays to stop Black from (eventually) establishing pawns on e5 and f5. Now Black plays to induce White to remove the cramping pawn on d5.

| 8. | ... | e5 |
| 9. | de6 | Bxe6 |
| 10. | b3 | |

10. *Qd3* is the other common way to defend c4. It is certainly playable; but the Queen may be harassed there by *...Na6-c5*, or by pawn-sac lines involving *...Ne4* (either now or after *10... Na6 11. Bf4*, e.g., then *11... Ne4!? 12. Nxe4 fe4 13. Qxe4 Bf5*) or *...Nc5!?* (see *Journal of a Chess Master*, Game 34).

White's *10. b3* is more solid, and it tempts a now unsound *...Ne4* sac — indeed, *White* sacks an exchange — *10... Ne4? 11. Nxe4 Bxa1 12. Qxd6 Qxd6 13. Nxd6 Bc8 14. Bg5* with a big advantage.

Black plays the best move.

| 10. | ... | Na6 |

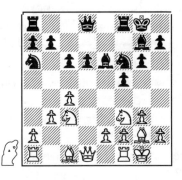

**11. Ba3?!**

Known to be bad — unfortunately, not known by Black. Note the clue: a3 and c3 are unprotected. That suggests *11... Qa5!?*, when Black wins an ex-

change in the "forcing" line *12. Qxd6 Rfe8 13. Bb2 Ne4 14. Nxe4 Bxb2 15. Neg5 Rad8*.

Better is the natural *11. Bb2*, with approximate equality. For an example of how a Virtuoso Master of the Leningrad Dutch handles the black pieces, observe please ... Lonoff–Gerzadowicz, 8th US CC Ch. Final: *11. Bb2 Kh8 12. e3 d5 13. cd5 Nxd5 14. Qc1 Qe7 15. Rfd1 Rfd8 16. Ne2 Nf6 17. Nf4 Bg8 18. Ne5 Qe8 19. Qc3 Nc7 20. Nxc6 Rxd1† 21. Rxd1 h6 22. Ne7 Nb5 23. Qe5 g5 24. Nfg6† Kh7 25. Qxf5 Qb8 26. Nf8† Kh8 27. Neg6#.*

White went on to tie for the title.

Black went on to write the tournament book — The Loser's Revenge.

| 11. | ... | Ne4? |

Possibly even worse than at Move 10, since the R/a1 is now protected.

| 12. | Nxe4 | fe4 |
| 13. | Nd4 | Qf6 |

*13... Bf5 14. Nxf5* is also good for White. Then *14... gf5 15. Qxd6* is similar to the game, though e4 is safer, while more fun is *14... Bxa1 15. Nh6† Kg7 16. Qxa1† Kxh6 17. Bc1 g5* (*17... Kh5 18. Qg7*) *18. h4*, when Knights and Rooks don't seem very important.

In what follows, Black's attack on a Rook is matched by White's attack on a Rook.

| | | |
|---|---|---|
| 14. | Nxe6 | Qxe6 |
| 15. | Qxd6 | Qxd6 |
| 16. | Bxd6 | Rfd8 |
| 17. | Rad1 | Rd7 |
| 18. | Bf4 | |

| | | |
|---|---|---|
| 18. | ... | Rad8 |

Dropping the e-pawn forthwith. But struggling to save it is awkward and I think ultimately futile, e.g., *18... Re7 19. Bg5 Re5 (19... Re6/8 20. Rd7) 20. h4 h6 (20... Nc5 21. b4 Ne6 22. Bc1! - b2) 21. Bf4 Re7 22. Rd6 Kf7 23. Rfd1* and White will seize the 7th rank.

| | | |
|---|---|---|
| 19. | Rxd7 | Rxd7 |
| 20. | Bxe4 | |

"And wins." Alas for White — if he did, the game wouldn't be in the book. But if a 1900-player can mess this up, that means there must be something here for most of us to learn.

| | | |
|---|---|---|
| 20. | ... | Nc5 |
| 21. | Bc2 | Ne6 |
| 22. | Rd1 | Rxd1† |

*22... Nd4?! 23. Kf1 e3.*

| | | |
|---|---|---|
| 23. | Bxd1 | Kf7 |
| 24. | Be3 | |

Some points ...

—White wants to exchange the B/e3 for the B/g7, or the B/d1 for the Knight. He does *not* want to swop the B/e3 for the Knight. He might then still be winning, but opposite-colored Bishops are notorious for giving drawing chances.

—There's no hurry. Some endings certainly must be calculated and played sharply; but here, what can Black do?

—Think Generally, especially since you *do* have that luxury of time. Such thinking is often particularly useful in playing endings. Thus — where do the white pieces belong? How about King in the center, Bishops on the long diagonals? What could be better? So — *B/d2, e3, f3, K/ d3 (b4 if necessary), f4, B/f3, B/ c3*. Then gently push Black off the back edge of the board.

—Find a Plan. If not the above, something. Don't just make moves.

| | | |
|---|---|---|
| 24. | ... | c5 |
| 25. | f4 | Nd4 |
| 26. | Bf2? | |

Not at once *Bd2-c3* because of *...Nxe2†*, but first *26. Kf2*, then if the Knight remains, *Bd2-c3* and *e3*, getting one of the desirable exchanges. If the Knight retreats, *Kd3, Bc3, e3, Bf3*, etc.

| 26. | ... | b6 |
| 27. | e3 | Nc6 |
| 28. | Be1 | Nb4 |

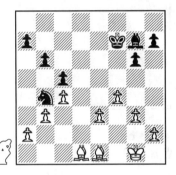

**29. Bxb4?**

*No!* 29. a3 wins. 29. a4 wins. 29. Kh1 wins! Even without the pawn on a2, two good Bishops and a passed pawn-plus is enough.

Now, it's much harder.

| 29. | ... | cb4 |
| 30. | Kf2 | Bc3 |

Mr. Lamansky: "My goal now was to put my pawns on black squares and keep my Bishop mobile."

| 31. | Kf3 | Kf6 |
| 32. | Bc2 | Bb2 |
| 33. | g4 | h6 |
| 34. | h4 | g5 |

With a 3-on-2 fastbreak in basketball or a power play in hockey, where do you want your players? S p r e a d   o u t! Don't let the other side cover two of your men with one of theirs. So

here? Spread out, separate your passed pawns — 35. fg5† hg5 36. h5! (36. hg5† wins, but why not have a passed h-pawn rather than a g-pawn?). Now Black would like to sit on e5 with his King, but he can't — 36... Ke5 37. Bf5 and next 38. h6, when Black must move his King to stop the pawn. White then plays Ke4, when ...

— If the black King is on d6, the black Bishop must cover h8, so White can play Bg6, Kf5xg5.

— If the black King is on f6, White can decisively advance his e-pawn (Kd5 if Bb2, Kd4 if Bc1 ... Bb2† Kd5, e3-e4).

The Long Arm of the black King doesn't reach from h8 to e5.

**35. hg5**
Harder still....

| 35. | ... | hg5 |
| 36. | Ke4?! | Bc1 |

Okay, let's think about this. Black won't play *g5xf4*, giving us *mobile* connected passed pawns. So White must do something.

But first — any hurry? Nah, *37. Bb1* wins. But since we *have* time, why not get our pieces as active as possible? Thus, *37. Kf3! 38. Bf5! 39. Ke4!* (give Black either King or Bishop moves, ending K/f6, Bishop wherever).

Now spread out: *40. fg5†* *Kxg5 41. Bc8.* As before, Black can't stop *e3-e4* (*Bc1, Kd4* or *Bb2, Kd5*). The best Black can do is K/f6 and B/b2, White, K/d5, P/e4, P/g4. But now White can play *e5†*, since *...Bxe5* loses the Bishop to *g5†*. So, Black must fall back — *...Ke7. Then* White plays *g5 Bc1; g6 Bh6; Bf5 Bg7; c5 bc5; Kxc5 a5!?; Kb5 Bxe5; Kxa5 Bc3; Ka4 Bd2; a3 ba3; Kxa3,* and White will win — the black King can stop one pawn, so the white King goes to the other, where the black Bishop will have to be sacked to stop its advance.

S p r e a d 'em out. Stay active. Go for the net.

**37. f5?**

Instead, we have two guys standing on the foul line with Pat Ewing in their face.

| 37. | ... | Bd2 |
| 38. | Kd4 | Bc3† |
| 39. | Kd5 | Bd2 |
| 40. | e4 | Bc3 |
| 41. | Kd6 | |

Holding e5. *41. Kc6 Bd4 42. Kb7 a5 43. Kc6 Ke5=.*

| 41. | ... | Bd4 |

| 42. | Kd5 | Bc3 |
| 43. | Bd1 | Be5 |

| 44. | c5 | |

What else?

| 44. | ... | bc5 |
| 45. | Kxc5 | Bc3 |
| 46. | Kd5 | Be5 |
| 47. | Kc4 | Bc3 |
| 48. | a4 | |

*48. a3 a5 49. Kb5 ba3* is not to be recommended.

| 48. | ... | Ke5 |
| 49. | a5 | Kf6 |
| 50. | Kd5 | Be5 |
| 51. | Be2 | Bc3 |
| 52. | Kd6 | Bd4 |
| 53. | Kd5 | Be5 |
| 54. | Kc6 | Bd4 |
| 55. | Kb5 | Bc3 |
| 56. | Kc4 | **Drawn** |

There's a technical chess-ending lesson here, and also a general, sporting one. Be tough. Hang in there. Do the best you can with what you've got. A lesser player would've given up on Black's position and not made things so difficult for White.

And lost.

## PART V — Attacks Good and Bad

*The idea of balance is enough to convince us that balanced positions with best play on either side must lead again and again to balanced positions. Only after the balance of the position has been disturbed, so that one player holds an advantage, may this player attack with intent to win.*

*One may err, but one must not deceive oneself. He who bravely follows his judgment may lose but even his loss profits him, provided he seeks to discover the reasons for it; and he grows to be a master, an artist. But he who no longer ventures to back his opinion loses the quality of fighter and approaches his fall.*
*—Emanuel Lasker*

Stonewall Martin is worthy of his illustrious namesake, who was famous for rapid flanking maneuvers.

### w: Floyd Sanger (1881)
### b: William Martin (1658)
Dutch Defense A85/5
## SANTA MONICA BAY CC RATING TNMT.

| | | |
|---|---|---|
| 1. | d4 | f5 |
| 2. | c4 | Nf6 |
| 3. | Nc3 | e6 |
| 4. | g3 | c6 |
| 5. | Bg2 | d5 |

Black's "Stonewall" setup is a bit single-minded. He takes a stand on the white squares, plans ...Ne4, a King-Bishop move, ...0–0, ...Qe8-h4, and a quick mate with ...Nd7-f6-g4 or ...g5, ...Rf6-h6, or a plan involving ...f4. If it were this easy, White wouldn't dare play 1. d4.

What's wrong with Black's idea? As quickly as he seized e4, he gave up e5. White often plays Bf4 and/or Nf3-e5, when Black must suffer White's Knight to remain there, or exchange it and see a cramping white pawn on e5. And, in general, pawns on c6, d5, e6, f5 *guarantees* that White will have dark squares to play on.

But note the difference—Black's Knight on e4 *can* be driven away. White has the option of f2-f3, perhaps even followed by e2-e4. Or not! The point is that White can still decide what his best setup is. "Theoretically," Black has made committal pawn decisions too soon.

*And* those pawns lock in his Queen's Bishop. A "problem piece," it sometimes gets out via d7-e8-g6 or -h5, sometimes winds up on a6 or b7. But often, it stays on c8, the Rook stays on a8, and Black tries to win without 'em. And often does! For all its defects, the Stonewall *is* dangerous. Its aim is checkmate; if White slips up, the penalty is more than usually fatal.

This opening is not all that common in current GM practice, but Nigel Short and Artur Yusupov, most notably, have won recent games with it.

**6. cd5?!**

Questionable. This helps Black. He recaptures with the e-pawn, when his grip on e4 is as strong as ever. And now "all" he has to do is play ...f4, and his problem Bishop is ready to join the attack. White has removed one of Black's own roadblocks.

Not only did the pawn on e6 block a diagonal, it blocked the e-file. Now if White drives a Knight off e4 with f2-f3, his e-pawn will be backward on an open file.

So why play 6. cd5? Perhaps White feared ...dc4. But he needn't have. After 6. Nf3 dc4 he could recover the pawn easily with Ne5xc4. But also good

would be 7. 0-0. Then look! Black has made five pawn moves, White, three. Black has one piece developed, White, three and has castled. With a lead in development such as this, White should open things up. The move that begs to be played is e2-e4. White could prepare this with Re1 or Qc2 or Ne5 or Bg5.

So White need not fear ...dc4. But even if he did, 6. b3 would be better than the text.

| 6. | ... | ed5 |
| 7. | Nh3 | Bd6 |
| 8. | Bf4 | 0-0 |
| 9. | a3 | a5 |

White planned a "Minority Attack," so called because he has three pawns versus four on the Queen's half of the board. Minority Attack is an old name, by the way. In a modern book, you'll find this listed under Affirmative Action.

The Plan was b2-b4-b5. If Black allows, White would capture on c6, when if ...bc6 Black would have a backward pawn on the open c-file. Otherwise—if ...cb5 or ...Nxc6 or ...c5— Black's d-pawn will be isolated and easy for White to attack: Nc3, Bg2, Qb3, Nf4 (or if ...Be6, Ng5).

9... a5 doesn't solve Black's problem forever. White could threaten b2-b4 again with Rb1.

But at least then Black would have the chance to open the a-file for his Rook.

How *should* Black meet this "Minority Attack"? Three ways:

- Decide to live with a weakness on c6.
- Decide to live with a weakness on d5.
- Meet *b2-b4* with *...b7-b5*, then quickly play *...Nbd7-b6-c4*, shielding the weak c-pawn from frontal attack. That's the sturdiest defense. Also the most time-consuming. Should Black do it? Depends. If he has little counterplay, Yes. But No if he is giving White more trouble than he is getting—trading c6 for g1 is always a good idea.

|  |  |  |
|---|---|---|
| 10. | 0-0 | Bxf4 |
| 11. | Nxf4 | Ne4 |

The Bishop on d6 had been stopping *b2-b4*. Now this Knight does—*12. b4? Nxc3*. Accordingly, White might now play *12. Qc2* to threaten *13. b4*.

|  |  |  |
|---|---|---|
| 12. | e3 | Qf6 |
| 13. | Rc1 | Nd7 |
| 14. | b3? |  |

Did it slip out of his fingers?!! There's no reason to touch this pawn if not to play *14. b4!*

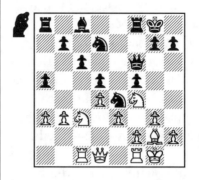

|  |  |  |
|---|---|---|
| 14. | ... | Qh6 |

Here he comes. And this offers a chance to again criticize *14. b3?* If White looks to blunt Black's initiative by exchanging Queens with *15. Qh5*, Black can take *15... Qxh5 16. Nxh5* and play *16... Nd2 17. Rfd1 Nxb3*. White doesn't lose a pawn—*18. Rb1 a4 19. Nxa4*—but Black has a big edge after *19... Rxa4 20. Rxb3 b5 △ ...Bb7, ...Nb6-c4, ...Rfa8.*

Or Black could answer *15. Qh5* with *...Qd6*, hitting a3, planning *...Ndf6* or *...Rf6-h6*.

All this works because of *14. b3? Do Not Make Unnecessary Pawn Moves*. A bad piece move can—if you're lucky—be undone. Pawn moves are forever.

|  |  |  |
|---|---|---|
| 15. | Na4 | Ndf6 |
| 16. | Nc5 | Nxc5 |
| 17. | Rxc5 |  |

*17. dc5 may* improve. The white Queen could be strongly centralized on d4.

Black's next is—eventually—a pawn sac, if White so chooses. He does.

Black's sac may not be justified. *You cannot win by a direct attack unless you have a winning advantage!* You cannot force your will upon a position. Does Black have much of an advantage here? I don't think so. He has a good Knight square in e4 and a bit of space on the Kingside; but he is behind in development (*B/c8! R/a8!*), and White's position is fundamentally sound.

Black should proceed "normally" with *17... Ne4, ...g5, ...Be6-f7-h5,* develop his Queen's Rook, and *then* eye White's King.

| 17. | ... | Ng4 |
|-----|-----|-----|
| 18. | h3 | Nf6 |
| 19. | Qe1 | |

*19. b4 (remember?) may still be worth a try. It looks to create a Black pawn weakness at minimal cost—Rook and pawn moves. Sending the Queen to a5 when Black is trying to storm the Kingside does not inspire confidence. I would not like to be White's insurance agent. But he may survive....*

| 19. | ... | g5 |
|-----|-----|-----|
| 20. | Nd3 | Ne4 |
| 21. | Rxa5 | Rxa5 |
| 22. | Qxa5 | f4 |
| 23. | ef4 | Bxh3 |
| 24. | fg5 | |

May be necessary. Black has two strong ideas:

*...g4, ...Bxg2, ...Qh3†, ...Nxg3, ...Qxg3†, ...Qh3†, ...g3;*

*...gf4 (Nxf4), ...Rxf4 (gf4), ...Qg6xg2.* Right *now,* this allows a perpetual; but White wants to resolve the situation.

| 24. | ... | Nxg5 |
|-----|-----|-----|
| 25. | Ne5 | Bxg2 |
| 26. | Kxg2 | Qh3† |
| 27. | Kg1 | Ne4 |
| 28. | Qe1 | |

Holds? If now *28... Rf6,* White has *29. Qe2 Rh6 30. Qg4†* or *29. Qa5 Rh6? 30. Qd8†* mating.

So how should Black continue? Queen, Rook, and Knight aren't getting it done; there's one guy left—*28... h5!?* Now if White tries *29. Qe2,* Black can at least equalize with *29... Rf5 △ 30... h4 31. Qg4† Qxg4 32. Nxg4 Rg5 (32... hg3? 33. Nh6†)* and Black will get his pawn back, with a draw likely.

Maybe White can stop the pawn with his Knight: *28... h5 29. Ng6 Rf7 (29... Rf5? 30. Ne7†.* When your opponent has an active Knight, be wary of putting two pieces on the same color it is sitting on.) *30. Nh4 Rg7*—nope—there's no good defense to *31... Qxh4*.

So Black seems to have enough for his pawn.

**28.   ...            b6**

But not this way. Black played this so that White could not answer *...Rf6-h6* with *Qa5-d8†* and a perpetual. But his notes show that he underestimated the *29. Qe2!* defense, intending *29... c5*. But White gets at least equal play, and maybe an edge, with *30. Qg4† Qxg4 31. Nxg4*, meeting *31... Nd2* with *32. Rd1, 31... h5* with *32. Ne5, 31... cd4* with *32. Rd1 h5 33. Ne5 Rxf2 34. Rxd4 Rd2*. And I have the feeling that there are more improvements for White than for Black in there.

**29.   Nxc6?**

After all our work; White misses the whole idea....

| | | |
|---|---|---|
| **29.** | **...** | **Rf6** |
| **30.** | **Ne7†** | **Kf7** |
| **31.** | **Nxd5** | **Rh6** |
| **32.** | **Resigns.** | |

One of the joys of my poetry library is a slim and precious tome, *The Dialogues of Athing*, by one Harold Holden. I didn't immediately connect him with this game but his letter's postscript gave it away—

*A canny old player of chess*
*When he found his positions a mess*
*Would manage to stumble*
*Sending pieces a-tumble*
*And enjoy his opponent's distress.*

### w: Harold Holden
### b: Jeff Barth
Nimzovich Defense B00/14
## NATIONAL CC TEAM CH.

| | | | |
|---|---|---|---|
| 1. | e4 | Nc6 | |
| 2. | d4 | d5 | |
| 3. | e5 | Bf5 | |
| 4. | Ne2 | e6 | |

Black has a French pawn structure, but has gotten his "problem" Bishop out before locking it in with ...e6. The Bad News is that the Knight on c6 is in the way of Black's thematic counter, ...c7-c5, to White's pawns on d4 and e5.

Here White can simply develop with 4. Nf3 or 4. Bb5, but the move he played seems more to the point. Ne2-g3 tried to make Black "pay" for his free and easy development.

| | | | |
|---|---|---|---|
| 5. | Ng3 | Bg6 | |
| 6. | Bd3 | | |

A bit inconsistent. He could pry a small concession out of Black with 6. h4. To that, Black has replied 6... f6, 6... h5, and 6... h6. The last is relevant to our game. After 6... h6 7. h5 Bh7 8. Bd3, Larsen says White has the upper hand. That's our position with the pawns on h5 and h6, increasing White's space advantage and restricting Black's options—he doesn't want his Rook on h7, so is pretty much forced to play 8... Bxd3.

**6. ... Nb4?!**

A cost/benefit analysis of this move is complicated, but I think Black pays too much for what he gets.

6... Nge7!? 6... Qd7!?

**7. Bxg6 hg6**

He does get the open h-file. That's good ... but not *that* good. White has the space advantage on that side, and does not lag in development. It's unlikely that a Black attack will succeed there.

On the downside, White gains time. 8. c3 is a move he would just as soon play anyway. Now he gets it "for free."

**8. c3 Na6**

Perhaps hoping to get in ...c5. 8... Nc6 is equally playable.

White's next takes ...0-0-0 out of Black's options and stops an immediate 9... c5. But *Nd2-f3* could be better. See next note.

**9. Qb3 Rb8**
**10. Qb5† c6**

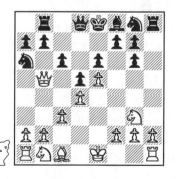

Because now *10... Qd7*

would be fine for Black. If White takes, the black King would be both safe and useful on d7. If White retreats, *11. Qe2,* say, he will have spent three Queen moves and not gotten much value for them, while Black is poised for the thematic *11... c5.* We'll do a similar accounting after Black's next.

Why is *...c7-c5* thematic? It attacks White's pawn chain at (or toward, actually) its base. What is the logic involved? Right now, White's pawns on c3, d4, and e5 are all protected by another pawn, and therefore generally safe from Black's pieces. The base at b2 is *not* protected by a pawn, but it's too hard for Black to get at. *...c7-c5* followed by *...cd4* brings the base up to d4, where it's easier to attack, e.g., *...Ne7-c6* (or *-f5*), *...Rh4, ...Rc8-c4.* Black may not win the pawn, but will make White spend time and effort defending it rather than having a free hand for *his* plans. Should White answer *...c5* with *dc5,* e5 is weakened and Black's pieces gain use of c5—particularly convenient here to get Black's mal-placed Knight off of a6.

Another point: every move, and every combination of moves, gains something and gives up something. Black's pawns on f7 and e6 are hard to get at; but then, Black has only extended his pawns to his 4th rank. He hasn't risked as much, hasn't gained as much. On the other hand, White has seized more space, but on venturing more, has risked more—his pawns are easier to attack; they're closer to Black!

That's why "thematic." If Black does not thus attack the pawns, White gets the cramping benefit of his pawn chain without paying the cost.

**11.  Qe2          Nh6**

In the past three moves, White has moved his Queen from d1 to e2 while Black has played ...Rb8, ...c6, and ...Nh6. White's motive was to eliminate the possibility of 0-0-0 by Black, but I don't think it was worth it. Black's King will be as safe in the center as on the Queenside, especially since he should play ...c5!

**12.  0-0          Qh4?**

*12... c5!*

Black is attacking because he *wants* to attack, but you can't just do that. You should do what the position allows, what it calls for.

What's wrong with *12... Qh4?* Black is attacking where he does not have an advantage. *White* has the Kingside space advantage. If there were a black

pawn on e4, Black's action would be justified. White would not have the obvious defense *Nd2-f3*. The open h-file is a factor, but without more of an advantage (space or development) Black's attack should not succeed.

A further note—if Black had played ...c5 and ...cd4, *then* ...Qh4 would be part of the thematic attack on d4! Checkmate is incidental. Think thematic.

| | | |
|---|---|---|
| 13. | Nd2 | Nf5 |
| 14. | Nf3 | Qd8 |
| 15. | Nxf5 | gf5 |
| 16. | Ng5 | Be7 |
| 17. | f4 | g6? |

Not good. Unnecessary. Without this move, Black could think about playing ...Nc7, ...Qd7, ...f6 and answering *ef6* with ...gf6, maintaining pawn control of e5. He might *not* do this, but there's no percentage in giving up the option without getting value in return. Here, he doesn't. What does *17... g6* do? Covers f5 in case White plays *g2-g4*, maybe; but that's not necessary until White plays the move—if then. Supports ...Rh5, maybe? Yes ... but that move is not so great that it's worth so compromising your pawn structure.

Black should prepare ...c5 (surprise) with *17... Qd7* or *17... Nc7*. He could even play it at

once—*17... c5 18. Qb5† Kf8* (if
*18... Qd7, 19. Qxd7† Kxd7 20.
Nxf7*)—when I think Black's
Queenside chances are more sig-
nificant than any danger to the
King on f8.

**18. b4**

After all I've said, I can't be
too critical of a move that stops
...c5! But still, I would prefer a
more positive plan immediately:
*18. Rf3, 19. Qd3, 20. Rh3*. Play
where you have the advantage.
***Don't play defense unless neces-
sary.***

**18. ... Nc7**

**19. Rf3 Bxg5?!**

There's no need to give up
this good Bishop, especially after
weakening f6 with *17... g6?* And
surely Black need not fear *20.
Rh3 Rxh3 21. Nxh3.* So why
eliminate the white Knight?

Black should not play on the
Kingside! Instead, *19... b6* and
...c5 or *19... a5!? 20. a3* (*20. ba5
Ra8*) *ab4 21. ab4 Ra8* should be
tried. This suggestion stays in ef-

fect for several moves.

| 20. | fg5 | Ke7 |
| 21. | Qf2 | Rh7 |
| 22. | h4 | a6 |

Perhaps a wise precaution.
Black plans *...Na8!?-b6-c4,* but
sees that on *22... Na8* White has
a dangerous-looking pawn sac in
*23. b5!* Its positional point is to
activate the locked Bishop with
*23... cb5 24. Ba3† Ke8 25. Bd6
Rc8 26. a4* with reasonable compensation.

After the text, White has an
interesting idea in *23. a4,* again
threatening the Bishop-freeing
b4-b5 sac. But Black might well
reply *23... b5,* when it's hard to
see the Bishop *ever* becoming a
factor in the game. If White
keeps the Knight out of c4 with
a4-a5, it could head for g7 (first
...Qg8 to cover f7 in case of
...Ng7; g2-g4). As long as Black
controls h4-h5, he couldn't lose;
the Bishop is just too bad. But
Black's winning chances would
also be slim.

Black may have a *slight* advantage—see next note. So, objectively best for White would be
to play for a draw with *23. a4!?*

| 23. | Bf4 | Na8 |
| 24. | Rh3 | Nb6 |
| 25. | Qf3 | Qg8 |
| 26. | Kf2 | |

*26. h5?! Rxh5 27. Rxh5 gh5
28. Qxh5 Qg6!* gives Black a big

advantage, as the Bishop will never be more than a big pawn. The pawn sac *28. g6* instead of *28. Qxh5* looks inadequate. White could prepare said sac with *Kf2-e2, g2-g4, Rg1*, but Black can eliminate all danger by: 1) stopping *h4-h5* with *...Rh5*, and 2) being able to meet *g2-g4* with *...fg4* by keeping f7 safe.

Then he can either look for Queenside play or offer a draw.

| 26. | ... | Qg7?! |
| 27. | Ke2 | Nc4 |
| 28. | Kd3 | Ra8 |
| 29. | Qe2 | Qh8?! |
| 30. | Rah1 | Qd8? |

Arrrgh. *30... Rh5!*

**31. h5**

Black could not have chosen a more unfortunate setup. If he ever captures with the g-pawn, *g5-g6* will threaten *Bg5!*

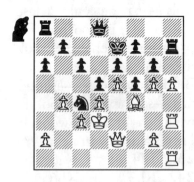

| 31. | ... | Rg7 |
| 32. | h6 | Rh7 |

Now a Pawn of Damocles hangs over Black's game. He must *always* watch the h-pawn. The problem is that while he is doing that, White may shift everything to the Queenside, where Black will be, in effect, a Rook down.

What is fascinating is that *Black* also has good Queenside prospects. His Knight is powerfully posted and invulnerable, and his Queen and Queen's Rook are placed to support *...a5!?* The only thing wrong with Black's Queenside play is the pawn on h6!

The difference in their fortunes is that White has good long-term chances and Black is poised for action now. Black's dilemma is that if his aggression on the Queenside doesn't *force* at least a draw, it will work mightily to his disadvantage. Then White will use the open lines, and Black will be hard-pressed to defend, since every exchange will favor White. The fewer the pieces, the bigger the h6-pawn.

With all this in mind, best now for White is to hurry to the Queenside with *33. Rb1* and *Rhh1*.

**33. Rf1?     Qb6?!**

This move is too slow. Or too fast!

As explained, if Black is going for Queenside play, he should go all out, As Fast As Possible. A

sample line: *33... a5! 34. a3 (34.
Rb1?! ab4 35. Rxb4 b6 △ ...Ra3,
...Qa8) ab4 35. ab4 Ra3 36. Rc1
Qa8 △ ...Qa4 and ...Ra2 or
...Qa6!?* and a discovered check;
or if *Rc1-c2, ...Ra1*. I don't think
Black can win with any of these,
but he does seem to have enough
activity to continually harass
White. Dynamic equality. I
*think*. Could be wrong. Tough to
analyze. *Maybe* White can con-
solidate enough to force exchanges. Then he wins. If it were
*my* postal game, I'd spend four or
five hours here. If it were an OTB
game, I'd go for it: *33... a5!* It's
easier to attack than defend.

But if calculation or caution
argues against that, Black should
close Queenside lines with *33...
b5*. Then he can either try to
neutralize the a-file with *...Nb6-
a4*, either before or after *a2-a4,
ab5 ab5*, or, worse but maybe possible, even allow *a4, Ra1-a2,
Rhh1-a1* and try to defend c6
with his two back ranks: *...Rc8-
c7, ...Rh8, ...Kf8-g8-h7*.

But I may be too severe. *33...
Qb6 might* give Black enough.
See next note.

**34. a4?**

No, no! Look where the
white pieces are. Look where
White pushes a pawn. To a4? His
King is the closest piece! We'll
see what's wrong with *34. a4* at
Move 37.

White should strive to keep
things closed with a line-block-
ing pawn sac: *34. Rb1 a5 35. b5!
cb5 36. Bc1 △ Kc2-d1-e1*, still
with good chances because of
*R/h7*.

But I may be missing something. Try to find a win for Black;
there may be one.

But the main point holds—
Black should *hurry* to play where
he is stronger; White should
strive to keep that area closed
until he can ship some troops
over there.

| 34. | ... | a5 |
|-----|-----|-----|
| 35. | Rb1 | ab4 |
| 36. | Rxb4 | Qa6 |
| 37. | Kc2 | b6? |

By now, we know that Black
should look at *37... b5!* That's in

general. Now we look at specific tactics to see if it works. This can obviously be done by pure number-crunching calculation, but we can be aided even here by general considerations. Here are two:

1) Resist "automatic" moves —recaptures and checks—so that you are alert to other possibilities.

2) Rather than plunging into a maze of variations or randomly selecting tries, look for a doubtless effective setup, and then see if there's a good way to get there.

Thus, here after *37... b5 38. ab5* don't look only at *38... cb5?!* We have Queen, Rook, and Knight, and want 'em *all* active. How? Where? Almost certainly, on White's first two ranks. Probably Q/a1 and R/a2. You can guess where we're heading, but I confess I tried *38... Qa2†* first. But after *39. Kd3* the best I could find is *39... Qa1!* So my check just gave White a free move. Obviously (now), Black should answer *38. ab5* with *38... Qa1* immediately. *Now* how does White defend against *...Ra2†?* By *39. Kd3* (!). But after *39... Ra2*, Black's three live pieces are ideally posted. After *40. Qf3 Qe1* △ *...Rf2* or *...Rd2†!*, I don't see how White survives.

Instead, Black heads straight for a Queen exchange, a mistake both tactically and positionally. The fewer the pieces, the bigger factor the R/h7.

**38. Be3        Na3†**

Black offered a draw here and on Moves 44, 51, and 56.

**39. Kd1        Qxe2†**
**40. Kxe2       Nc4**
**41. Rh1        Kd7**
**42. Bf4        Kc7**
**43. Kf3**

Here we can see the problem for Black on the h-file. He can achieve a modest success on the Queenside with *43... c5 44. dc5 bc5 45. Rhb1 Rxa4*, but after *46. Rb8* △ *Rg8, Rb1-b8-f8, Rg7*, White will make a Queen.

**43. ...         Kb7**
**44. g4**

If Black allows *g4xf5*, whichever pawn he captures with will allow White to eventually push the now-freed opposite number. Black's best remedy for that would be to play *...ef5* and *...Ke6*. But then White wins by putting his Rooks on a1 and b1 and playing *Bc1* △ *Ba3-b4, a4-a5*. This could allow *Ba3 Rxa4*, but *Bb4* is still winning; a white Rook will penetrate (△ *Bb4* and *Re7!*).

In what follows, the *Ra1, Rb1, Bc1-a3-b4* idea remains good, if not to play *a5*, then (once *Bb4*) to double on the f-file. Black can't both protect f7 and stop the h-pawn, as black Rooks on b7 and h7 allow *Bf8-g7!*

| 44. | ... | fg4 |
| 45. | Kxg4 | Ka6 |
| 46. | Ra1 | Rb8 |
| 47. | Kf3 | Rb7 |
| 48. | Ke2 | Ka5 |
| 49. | R4b1 | Rh8 |
| 50. | Kf3 | Rh7 |
| 51. | Ra2 | Ka6 |
| 52. | Bc1 | Rh8 |
| 53. | Ke2 | Rhc8 |
| 54. | R2a1 | Ra7 |
| 55. | Rb3 | Rca8 |
| 56. | Ba3 | Nxa3 |

Else *Bb4*, *Rf1* and *-f2* ...

| 57. | R1xa3 | Kb7 |
| 58. | Rb4 | Kc7 |
| 59. | Rab3 | Rb8 |
| 60. | Kd3 | Rab7 |
| 61. | c4 | **Resigns.** |

Why now? White is winning, but there's a lot of work yet. I think White's best setup is R/c3, R/c2, K/b4. Black must cover c6 twice. Then White plays his Rooks to f3 and f2. Black can't cover f7 with ...*Rb7*, ...*Rc8*, ...*Ke8* because the h-pawn goes in. So he must banish a Rook to h7. A variation on this theme is to play *Rh2* and *h6-h7*, when Black must play ...*Rh8*.

In either case, White then plays a quick *a4-a5* and penetrates with King and Rook, with a more mobile second Rook ready to swing over.

So why resign now? Prejudice against slow torture, perhaps.

Mr. Capron shows he would score well indeed on a chess IQ test. Would you?! Here's your chance to find out.

## Mark Capron (1426)–Arthur Dupee (1477)
B15/4(20)
### USCF CC TNMT. 1992-93

1.   e4        g6
2.   d4        Bg7
3.   Nf3      c6
4.   Nc3      d5

*4... d6* would make it a Pirc Defense.

After *4... d5* we have an off-beat variation of the Caro-Kann, also often reached by *1... c6, 2... d5*.

5.   e5       Nh6

Given that White just locked the d-pawns, Black might get his Bad Bishop out with *5... Bg4*.

6.   h3       0–0
7.   Bf4

Threatening to win a piece with *8. Qd2 Nf5 9. g4*.

7.   ...       f6
8.   Qd2     Nf7
9.   0–0–0

By transposition, we have Czerniak–Hernando 1975. Czerniak now suggests *9... Na6!* △ *...Nc7-e6* as equal. A slightly unusual maneuver, but suggested by the pawn structure. The square in front of an advanced or passed pawn beckons to enemy Knights, particularly when the Knight can't easily be driven away by a neighboring pawn. From that blockading square, a Knight attacks the blockadee's pawn (and here, Bishop!) defenders, and rules out unpleasant surprises such as *9... Nd7? 10. e6*.

9.   ...      Na6
10.  Bxa6

Defines much of the coming struggle, but maybe not best. Certainly this is not as good an idea as was *...Bg4xf3*. The difference? This is White's *good* Bishop; it belongs on d3, attacking the light squares g6 and h7 in conjunction with *h4-h5*.

But *10. Bxa6* is not terrible by any means. After *10... ba6* White has one of the world's great Knight squares in c5. Not only is it safe from black pawns, it is awkward for the black Knight or King's Bishop to challenge that outpost. And the black a-pawns are undeniably weak. But in a funny way *White* has devalued them, so they are a less appealing target for him! It would be more important for White to win a pawn on b7 than on a6. Of course in effect White has already "won" the pawn on b7 — c6 is weak, and c5 is secure from *...b6*.

But this situation has positive features for Black too — the open file and the two Bishops. The file is pure profit, the Bishops less clearly so. If the position stays closed, they are no advantage at all.

> **10.    ...         ba6**
> **11.    Rde1**

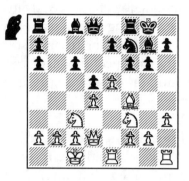

**11.    ...         e6**

Are you sure? *You* — could you be sure this is good? Here's a Very General Rule — if you're not sure what to move, move a piece, not a pawn. If it doesn't turn out so red-hot, you may be able to repair the damage with a discreet retreat.

I suggest *11... Qa5*, both to slow down White's *Na4-c5* and to allow *...Nd8-e6* (still a great square).

Perhaps Black played *11... e6* to stop *12. e6*, but that would not be all that good for White. Black would have a fine reply in *12... Nd6*, or if *11... Qa5, 12... Nd8*, when the pawn on e6 looks a goner.

And *11... e6* gives up on getting the Queen's Bishop out, e.g., after White's next (*12. h4*), wouldn't *12... Bg4* be nice?

> **12.    h4          h5**

g6 would be weak in any case after *13. h4-h5*. This at least keeps the h-file closed.

But one Joy of a space advantage lies in being able to play on a broad front, shifting troops faster than the cramped opponent can respond, or otherwise induce concessions.

**13. Na4       f5**

Thus here. On an ideal board, Black would like to keep pressure on e5; but after *Nc5* White is bearing down on a6 and e6, with *ef6* and *Qe2* in the offing.

And activating his Knight with *...Kh7, ...Nh6-f5* appeals — but White has too much space and activity, e.g., *13... Kh7 14. Nc5 Nh6 15. ef6 Qxf6 16. Ng5† Kh8 17. Ncxe6 △ Be5*. The more closed the position, the less likely stuff like this is.

**14. Rh3**

An unusual way to activate this Rook, but very strong. Good non-routine thinking by White.

Now Black should consider *14... Rb8!* This move was not possible when White had *e5xf6*

as a reply, but now it looks good. That Rook is Black's least active piece, and it's hard to imagine that it will find a better square than b8 any time soon.

**14. ...       Qe7**
**15. Rg3       Kh7**
**16. Nc5       Bh6**

Again, *16... Rb8!?*

After the text, White trades Bishops and settles in with *Ng5†*. Maintaining his Knight on f7 gives Black the option of *...Kh8* or *...Nxg5*.

**17. Bxh6       Nxh6**
**18. Ng5†       Kg7**
**19. Qa5**

This is like watching tennis — White nimbly shifts from side to side. Mr. Capron points out the threat *Nxa6, Rb3, Nc7*. That's hard to meet while continuing to hold e6. (Wouldn't *19... Rb6* be nice now?)

I like Black's next, getting a good square for his Knight.

**19. ...       f4**
**20. Rb3       Nf5**
**21. Nxa6**

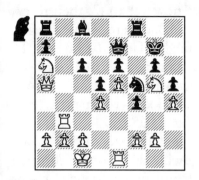

Now Black's Knight has a choice of pawns. What do you think? h4 or d4?

He takes on h4. That has the point of threatening White's Knight on g5, but I think *21... Nxd4* may be better. Always look to the center! There's no guarantee, but centralization increases options increases chances of a good option. On *21... Nxd4*, if White wants to keep his Rook on the b-file we have *22. Rb4*, when Knight retreats are bad — *22... Nb5 23. a4* or *22.. Nf5 23. Nc7*. But Black can use the occasion to exchange White's dangerous Knight — *22... Bxa6 23. Rxd4 (23. Qxa6? Qxb4) Bc8 (23... c5? 24. Qxc5!)*, when White has the better minor piece — and game — but Black may find sufficient counterplay with ...c5.

And *21... Nxd4 22. Rd3 Nf5 (△ ...Nxh4!)* looks okay for Black.

| 21. | ... | Nxh4 |
| 22. | Qc7 | |

*22. Nf3* looks equal, if double-edged, while White wants no part of *22. Nc7? Qxg5 23. Nxa8 f3†*.

After *22. Qc7* Black should probably play *22... Re8*. Then after *23. Qxe7 Rxe7 24. Nc5 (24. Rb8 Rxb8 25. Nxb8 is peculiar — the N/b8 is awkward for both players after 25... Rc7 or 25... Bb7) Nxg2 25. Rg1 Nh4 26. Rh3 Nf5 27. c3*, White can pick up f4 at will and have strong pressure against e6 and g6, e.g., with *Nd3xf4†*. That would be hard for Black to hold, but it's better than the text.

| 22. | ... | Bd7 |

Walking into a pin. The Reader is invited to enjoy speculating on white Knights visiting c5 and e6 and the consequences thereof. Thus *23. Nc5!*, when *23... Qxg5 24. Nxe6†* is a glorious fork, and *23... Rfd8 24. Ngxe6†* only a little less so. *23. Rb7* looks equally crushing (*23... Rfd8 24. Nc5*).

Instead, White goes for a flashier solution which may not be as good.

| 23. | Nxe6† | Qxe6 |
| 24. | Nc5 | Qc7 |
| 25. | Qxd7 | |

Here *25. e6* looks better. White can play *Qe5†*, then take the Bishop with the pawn or Knight.

| 25. | ... | Qxd7 |
| 26. | Nxd7 | Nxg2 |

No better is *26... Rf7 27. e6 Re7 28. Nb8!*, when c6 goes (*28... Rc7 29. e7*).

| 27. | Rg1 | Rfd8 |
| 28. | Nf6 | **Resigns.** |

*28... Nh4 29. Nxh5† and 30. Nxf4.* Nimble stepping by the white Knights!

So how did *you* do anticipating the Knight moves and threats? See everything in a flash? If not — or even if so — try your hand at the ...

## CHESS IQ TEST

Your task is to move the Knight from a1 to b1 to c1 ... to every square along the first rank to h1, then up to h2 and back across to a2, up to a3, over to h3, zigzagging thus all the way to a8. *But* you must not land on a square occupied or controlled by a black pawn. So from h2 you must next get to f2, then to c2, a2, a3, b3, d3, etc. Thus to begin, you might play *Na1-c2-a3-b1*. To c1 is longer — *Nb1-a3-c2-a1-b3-c1*. And any route is okay as long as you dodge the pawns, e.g., *Nb1-a3-c4-a5-b3-c1*.

The idea is to do this, a1-a8, as quickly as possible. So get a clock and, alas, a friend to count any errors — you add ten seconds for every mistake (*Ne5??*).

When you've finished, take a break, then try it again.

What good is this? Even by IQ testing standards, this is a *rough* measure. I think it has value mostly as a workout, training in recognizing Knight patterns. And if your second try was much faster than your first, you clearly learned something!

The first try is claimed to be the better measure of actual skill, but the correlation is not a fine one.

But it *may* be worth something. Many years ago, this test was given to a large national sample of school children in Czechoslovakia who played chess. Four little kids did notably better than all the rest. Three of them were named Kavalek, Jansa, and Smejkal, now all GMs. And the very best of the lot was — Vlastimil Hort, the strongest Czech player of his generation.

And how long should a talented player take to run this maze? Hort took two minutes, his little friends three and a half, some current IMs took under three and a half, many took more. Miro Radojcic says, "According to believers ... under 5 minutes [and] you are probably a potential international player...; less than 4 minutes may make you a budding GM." (*Chess Life*, Dec. 1971, p. 709.)

By all means, use it for training — but don't quit your day job.

Probasco Precision and Dash return us to the days when Cochrane stalked the Highlands.

## w: Bob Probasco (2155)
## b: Frank Baker (2275)
Petroff Defense C42/5
## 1989 USCF Golden Knights Finals

| 1. | e4 | e5 |
|----|-----|-----|
| 2. | Nf3 | Nf6 |
| 3. | Nxe5 | d6 |
| 4. | Nxf7 | |

The Cochrane Gambit.

*John Cochrane (1978-1878), Scottish player, barrister, called to the bar in 1822. If the so-called romantic style existed then Cochrane has a claim to be regarded as its founder. A dashing player, he attacked at all costs often sacrificing pieces with abandon....*
— The Oxford Companion to Chess

Of Cochrane's Gambit, Howard Staunton wrote in his *Chess Practice* (1860):

*This opening is essentially different from other similar openings in which a piece is sacrificed for the success of the attack. Here the Knight sacrifice does not serve an immediate straightforward attack, but after quiet and gradual development of his forces White, eventually, has to obtain a favorable position.*

Bronstein is the Gambit's most illustrious advocate; IM Vitolinsh has made it part of his repertoire.

| 4. | ... | Kxf7 |
|----|-----|------|
| 5. | d4 | Be6 |

Whatever its other merits, this gambit gets us out of the books fast. *ECO* looks at only three moves here—

5... Nxe4? 6. Qh5† (△ 6... Ke7 7. Qe2 △ Bg5†);

5... Be7 6. Nc3 Re8 7. Bc4† "unclear";

5... g6, giving the game Vitolinsh–Anikaev 1979 as equal after *6. Nc3 Bg7 7. Bc4†* *Be6 8. Bxe6† Kxe6 9. f4 Kg7 10.* *e5 Re8 11. 0-0 Nc6 12. d5 de5* *13. dc6 Qd1 14. Nd1 bc6.* But pencil in that White was better with *12. ef6 Qxf6 13. Nb5 Re7* *14. c3* in Vaiser–Vysotsky cc. 1981-84.

The best treatment of this opening I know of is a 12-page theoretical article by Osnos and Kalinichenko in *New in Chess* *Yearbook 19.* Additional fifth moves they look at are *...b5?!,* *...Qe7?!, ...Bg4, ...d5, ...c6,* *...Nbd7,* and *...Qe8.* But they don't consider *5... Be6,* nor does that move occur in their lines with *5... g6,* Black's next move here.

Why do you suppose *5... Be6* is avoided? Probably because Black anticipates *f2-f4* and a White pawn storm, when the Bishop will be forced to move again.

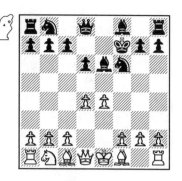

*after 5... Be6*

| 6. | Nc3 | g6 |
|----|-----|-----|
| 7. | Bd3 | Kg7 |
| 8. | 0-0 | Nbd7?! |

Mr. Probasco: "Black is starting to go wrong. He'll have time to challenge the center later — right now he needs to develop the Kingside by *...Be7* and *...Rf8.*"

Exactly right. Black may have a forest/tree problem. What he's doing *is* a good idea in itself, but should not be First Priority. In any position, but especially when you've just accepted a sacrifice, the Prime Directive is: Don't Get Mated. (Actually, that's a big part of the Prime Directive in *Star Trek* too, but they have to euphemize on prime TV.)

|    |    |    |
|----|-----|-----|
| 9. | f4  | c5? |

Again, *9... Be7* looks right.

|     |      |    |
|-----|------|-----|
| 10. | e5!? |    |

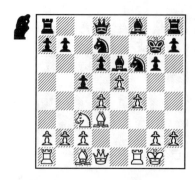

The bulk of the analysis that follows is by Mr. Probasco. In such a sharp position, tactics must predominate.

I will try to give the general, foresty thinking that could help structure, outline the calculations.

Thus here, how is White likely to follow up after Black's Knight moves? The move that cries out to be played is *f4-f5*, opening lines for the B/c1 and R/f1 and loosening up the black King's cover. With that in mind, Black should try now *10... de5*. The point is that after *11. de5*, when (if) White plays *f4-f5* Black will have *...Nxe5* in many variations.

So I certainly agree with Mr. Probasco — "He had to try *10... de5*, e.g., *11. de5 Nd5 12. Nxd5 Bxd5 13. Bxg6 Bxg2 14. Bf5*."

But in *this* position, I don't see a defense for Black. Instead of *13... Bxg2* I think Black should play *13... hg6 14. Qxd5 Qc7* or

*14... Nb6* or *14... c4!?* Δ *...Rxh2!*, *...Qh4†*, *...Bc5†*.

| 10. | ... | Nd5? |
| 11. | f5! | Nxc3 |

Mr. Probasco: "*11... gf5 12. Nxd5 Bxd5 13. Bxf5* is even worse, with one more piece for the attack and pressure on h7. *11... Bg8 12. f6† N5xf6 13. ef6† Nxf6* may be tenable." Though Black lags severely in development, e.g., *14. Qe1* Δ *Qh4* and *Bg5* or *Bh6†!?* and *Bc4†*.

Also, on *11... Bg8* White can remove a black Knight, then play *f6†* thus: *12. Nxd5 Bxd5 13. f6† Kg8 14. Qg4* Δ *Bxg6* (*14... Bf7? 15. e6; 14... Qe8 15. Bf5* Δ *Bg5, Rae1*).

**12. Qg4!?**

Mr. Probasco — "More forcing than *12. bc3.*"

Bravo. White resists the automatic recapture. It is pretty easy to see that this is plausible — after White moves his threatened Queen, Black still has two pieces attacked. Then he must decide if the move is *good*. Again, you would suspect so — Bg5 is now in the cards, as is a Queen shift to the h-file. Hey, the Queen is just *closer* to the action.

Then you work out the details.

**12.    ...                Bxf5?!**

Mr. Probasco: "Black can't keep his material advantage without allowing White to blow open the position, e.g.,

"*12... Bd5 13. Bh6† Kxh6 14. f6;*

"*12... Bf7 13. Bh6† Kg8 14. fg6;*

"*12... Ne2† 13. Bxe2 Bd5 14. c4 Bg8 15. f6†;*

"*12... de5 13. fe6 Nf6 14. Rxf6 Qxf6* (Had White played *12. bc3?!*, Black would do better with this line.) *15. Bg5 Ne2† 16. Kh1 Qf2 17. de5.*

"The best approach is to give the material back, although even here White is better, e.g.,

"*12... Nxe5 13. de5 Bc8 14. e6;*

"*12... Nd5 13. fe6 N7f6 14. ef6† Nxf6 15. Qh4;*

"*12... cd4 13. fe6 Nxe5 14. Qxd4.*"

| 13. | Bxf5 | Ne2† |
|-----|------|------|
| 14. | Qxe2 | gf5  |
| 15. | Rxf5 |      |

Black is in trouble. White threatens 16. Qg4†. Mr. Probasco gives:

"*15... Qh4 16. Rf4 Qe7 17. Qg4†;*

"*15... h5 16. Rg5† or 16. e6* followed by *Rg5†.*"

**15.    ...                Rg8**

Now of course 16. Qg4† Kh8 leads nowhere. How else can White continue? Attacking h7 twice suggests itself — *Qh5, Rf7, Qxh7* — but Black has time for *...Kh8* and *...Rg7*.

So what would you look at?

Developing a piece should *always* be considered....

**16.    Bg5!**

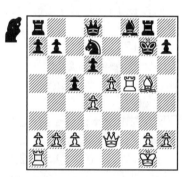

**16.    ...                Be7**

Mr. Probasco: "If *16... Qb6, 17. e6* threatening *Rf7†*, or *Bf6†* if the Knight moves.

"Black can try pinning the e-pawn against White's Queen by *16... Qe8*, but then *17. Bf6†* wins —

"*17... Kf7 18. Qc4†;*

"*17... Kh6 18. Qe3† Kg6 19.*

*Qg5† Kf7 20. Be7†;*

"17... Nxf6 18. ef6† Kh6 (18... Kh8 19. Qxe8 Rxe8 20. f7 or 18... Kf7 19. Qh5† Rg6 20. Qxh7† Ke6 21. f7) 19. Qd2† Kg6 20. f7."

**17. Qh5**

Now White threatens *Rf7†* and if *17... Kh8* first, he can still play it with tempo — *18. Bxe7 Qxe7 19. Rf7!*

Mr. Probasco notes that the other try, *17... Qe8*, fails to *18. Rf7† Qxf7 19. Bh6†.*

| 17. | ... | Rf8 |
| 18. | Bh6† | Kh8 |
| 19. | Bxf8 | Nxf8 |

Mr. Probasco takes us to the end: "*19... Bxf8 20. Rf7 Bg7 21. Qg4.*"

**20. Rf7**

"White threatens *Qh6.*"

| 20. | ... | Bg5 |

**21. e6**

"White also wins with *21. Raf1 Be3† 22. Kh1 Bxd4 23. Qh6!* or *21. Rxf8† Qxf8 22. Qxg5,* but this looked stronger. Besides, I couldn't resist the opportunity to offer a passive Queen sacrifice on move 23."

| 21. | ... | Be3† |
| 22. | Kh1 | Qg5 |

**23. e7!**     **Qg8**

"23... Qxh5 24. Rxf8† Kg7 25. Rxa8."

**24. Qf5**     **Bh6**

"24... Nd7 25. Rf1 and the mate threat wins the Knight, i.e., if 25... N-any, 26. Qf6†."

**25. dc5**

"Rather than cashing in immediately, White picks up more passed pawns. Black can't prevent it, since *25... dc5 26. Qe5† Bg7 27. e8=Q* is an easy win."

| 25. | ... | Ng6 |
| 26. | cd6 | Bg7 |
| 27. | Rf1 | Resigns |

Mr. Matthaey sings the old song, "What a difference a move makes . . ."

**w: Stephen Matthaey (1473)**
**b: Ernest Johnson (1995)**
Alekhine's Defense B02/17
## US Amateur Team Ch. 1993

| 1. | e4 | Nf6 |
|----|-----|------|
| 2. | e5 | Nd5 |
| 3. | Nc3 | Nxc3 |
| 4. | bc3 | d6 |
| 5. | f4 | g6 |
| 6. | d4 | Bg7 |
| 7. | Nf3 | b6 |

Lots of moves look better.

7... 0–0!? is most obvious. Black is certain to castle Kingside anyway. Do it now, then decide where to develop the pieces when you have more information (White's next move!). 7... Bf5 now or earlier is okay.

What's wrong with 7... b6? First, that move is not necessary to develop the Queen's Bishop. Black could well play ...Bf5 or ...Bg4. b7 is a fine square, but it is not clear that it is worth an extra developing move to post the Bishop there.

Second, ...b6 weakens the white squares. The pawns on a7, b6, c7, and d6 leave a6 and c6 without possible pawn protection. This is not necessarily fatal, but it is a liability Black need not assume. For example, combinations can occur with Bb5, d5, Nd4-c6. Black can stop such stuff, but he must remain alert to it, and must develop his forces with such ideas in mind. With the pawn on b7, Black is much more likely to have the option of ...c6.

This thinking is reflected in many common openings. In a Sicilian Dragon and King's Indian Defense, for example, Bg7 is combined with ...d6, while with a B/b7 Black commonly plays

...e6, as in the Nimzo-Indian and Queen's Indian, when the King's Bishop is usually developed on e7 or b4.

| 8. | Bd3 | 0–0 |
| 9. | 0–0 | e6 |

Now he weakens some dark squares! But he likely didn't like the look of 9... *Bb7 10. f5!?*

| 10. | Be3 | Bb7 |
| 11. | Qe1 | |

| 11. | ... | Nd7 |

This is okay, but *11... Nc6* may be better. From there the Knight could go to e7, and then to d5 or f5.

Another idea is *11... c5*, to try to dissolve the white pawn wedge or at least play on the c-file with ...cd4, ...Nc6, ...Rc8, and ...Na5-c4.

Without one of these plans, Black will be limited to passive defense.

| 12. | g4 | Qe8 |
| 13. | Qg3 | f6 |

Probably necessary sooner or later. *Ng5, ed6, Ne4* could be strong for White. Or *Rae1, Bd2, f4-f5.*

...*f7-f6* gives Black a *little* more room to organize a defense, and forces White to move his cramping pawn on e5. It is attacked four times and defended four times, but the defender on f3 may be eliminated at will.

| 14. | ed6 | cd6 |
| 15. | Rae1 | Bxf3 |

*15... Rc8* at once looks better. Taking the Knight may or may not be good, but for sure the decision could be postponed. The Knight doesn't have any immediate prospects. When it does look as if it might threaten something, *then* Black could take it off.

| 16. | Rxf3 | Rc8 |
| 17. | Bd2 | Qf7 |

Threatens *18... f5* freeing his Bishop and blunting the White attack. At once *17... f5 18. gf5 gf5 19. d5* is good for White. With the Queen on f7, Black can recapture on f5 with the e-pawn.

| 18. | f5 | e5 |
| 19. | fg6 | hg6 |
| 20. | Qh4 | Rfe8 |

Preparing his next, else *Rh3* and *Qh7*.

| 21. | Rh3 | Nf8 |
| 22. | Rf1 | e4 |

It is useful to get the Bishop away from g6 and h7.

| 23. | Bb5 | Re7 |

**24. Bf4**

*24. Bh6* at once may be better. By the time it is played, Black has "found" a slightly better defensive setup. But the Black idea suggested then would still work.

Now, Black must defend the d-pawn. He wastes a move with ...*Qd5-e6*, missing the idea *Ba4-b3*.

| 24. | ... | Qd5 |
| 25. | Ba4 | Qe6 |
| 26. | Bh6 | |

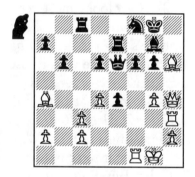

Now Black misses a *zwischenzug*, an in-between move, and loses quickly—26... Bxh6? 27. Rxf6.

How to avoid such mistakes? The thinking "I take his Bishop, he takes mine" is hard to resist, but you must try to develop the habit of looking at each position afresh. And *zwischenzugs* are often checks or attacks on an important piece by a less valuable one. *And*, given that backward pawns on an open file are traditional weaknesses, the f6-square fills one's vision.

The trick is to develop the alertness you need to spot such things. How? The short answer is—Practice!

Specifically ...

- Play a section of postal chess, and play it deliberately, as a training exercise. List *all* candidate moves, and why you reject those not played.

- Annotate some of your games, for publication if possible, or if not, for *serious* checking by a friend or teacher. This and postal chess both encourage you to work harder than you would in a casual postmortem analysis session.

- When you play over games for pleasure and profit, seek out those by *lower*-rated players, and look for mistakes. Work at this! Games between GMs aren't very useful. Those guys, almost without thinking, avoid the mistakes that *decide* most games between us mortals. We get a lot more to think about watching a C-player battle an A-player. Hey—that's how *we* play, that's what we need to learn about. You don't jump to 2600. You climb up, one rating point at a time. Start now.

• Take lessons. A good teacher can really accelerate your chess growth.

• Buy more great Thinkers' Press books, like those by Purdy, Dunne, Mengarini, and the Polish fellow with the long name.

Back to the business at hand. The move 26… Bxh6? fatally neglects f6. Can we cover f6 with the King if we allow 27. Bxg7 Kxg7? Looks shaky. White plays 28. Qh8† Kf7, and now diverts the black Queen away from that key f6-square with 29. Bb3 d5 30. Bxd5! Qxd5 31. Rxf6† and 32. Rxf8†, 33. Rxc8.

How else can we save f6? Well, it is attacked from f1 and h4. Can we block one of those lines? Ah—26… g5! A counter-in-between move—*gegenzwischenzug!* (Don't bother looking that up. I just patched it together.) White must move his Queen (The counter-counter … 27. Bb3 doesn't work—and my German couldn't stand it.).

If he plays 27. Qh5, he runs afoul of 27… Bxh6 (what a difference a move makes) 28. Qxh6 Rh7 29. Rxf6 Rxh6 30. Rxe6 (else …Qxg4†) Rxh3—avoiding the Bishop pin.

So after 26… g5 White must retreat with 27. Qg3 or 27. Qf2. It's complicated, but with 27… Ng6 △ …Nf4 I think Black holds. 27. Qf2 looks most testing. After 27… Ng6 28. Bxg7 Kxg7 there's no pin—29. Bb3 Qxg4†. But if White tries to use that Bb3 idea first, we get 27. Qf2 Ng6 28. Bb3 d5 29. Bxd5 Qxd5 30. Bxg7 Rxg7! 31. Qxf6 Rf8.

Am I missing anything? Who knows?! See what *you* can find.

But the Big Point is that Alertness and General Considerations led us to 26… g5!? Then we test it tactically, based in large part on ideas from our general considerations. I'm not *sure* it works, but it's a lot better try than the move in the game.

**26. … Bxh6?**
**27. Rxf6 g5**

What a difference a move makes …

**28. Qxh6 Qxg4†**
**29. Rg3 Resigns.**

Twenty-five years ago, if you asked me what I wanted to be when I grew up I might well have said, "Bud Lester." He wrote with wit and charm and grace, and I learned that a little humor never hurt a piece of chess writing. We mourned when he moved from Massachusetts to Maine, grieved when Utah lured him further.

When I got Savage-Djuric, I thought, well, we'll use it if it's good enough. But as soon as I knew we had a Lester game, I told Bob — "It goes in the book!"

### w: Alex Herrera
### b: Orlando Lester
Two Knight's Defense C59/3(15)
## LAS VEGAS TOURNAMENT, JAN. 1990

| 1. | e4 | e5 |
|----|-----|-----|
| 2. | Nf3 | Nc6 |
| 3. | Bc4 | Nf6 |

Discussion of this move could fill a book thicker than this one.

There's a Great Divide here — 4. d4 or 4. Ng5.

**4. Ng5**

Was 3... Nf6 that bad? Is this? No, and no.

Black responds as classically prescribed, in the center, and we enter one of the most analyzed of lines. Black sacks a pawn for Time and Space.

| 4. | ... | d5 |
|----|-----|-----|

| 5. | ed5 | Na5 |
|----|-----|-----|
| 6. | Bb5† | c6 |
| 7. | dc6 | bc6 |
| 8. | Be2 | h6 |
| 9. | Nf3 | e4 |
| 10. | Ne5 | |

Now Black has played 10... Bc5 and 10... Qc7. Most common is 10... Bd6 11. d4. Then there's Black's choice in our game, which, among other things, certainly stops 11. d4.

**10. ... Qd4?!**

Mr. Lester: "Needless to say, I wouldn't play this line in correspondence chess. I wouldn't even play it in OTB chess, but when you are in Las Vegas, gambling is not only legal but almost obligatory."

**11. f4**

*11. Ng4 Nxg4 12. Bxg4 Bc5 13. 0-0 (13... e3!?) works out as better for Black.*

**11. ...          Bc5**
**12. Rf1**

Now threatening *13. c3, 14. b4*. Black has played *12... Qd8±*, but has had more success with *12... Bb6*.

**12. ...          Bb6**
**13. c3          Qd6**

And here Kopylov–Bondarevski 1951 went *14. b4 Nb7 15. Na3!±. Nac4* will gain more time and, as importantly, cover the sensitive e3-square. White might (have?!) continue(d) *Bb2* and *Qc2, Qb3*, or *Qa4* (here gaining more time with the idea *Nxb6*), then *0-0-0*, and *then d3 or d4*.

For the next many moves, the pawn count is very much beside the point. Black has declared that he doesn't care about pawns. He let one go for room to swing his arms around. He wants a barroom brawl, a slugfest in open spaces, a chance to throw a Big Punch. Just look at those black pieces. Put the Bishop on e6 and a Rook on d8, and he's ready to rumble. Looks like a Young Ali.

Now look at White. Yep, just like all those white heavyweights — slow and ponderous and seemingly no danger to anybody. In a word, underdeveloped.

(Saying this is very Politically Incorrect. The White Heavyweight Anti-Defamation League is doubtless picketing CHESSCO even as you read this. But, hey, I'm just *telling it like it is*.)

White has to build himself up before he can take this guy on. And *not* stick his chin out. *14. b4* is best, but even *14. Na3* at once looks better than the text.

An extra pawn is nice, but you have to survive to enjoy it. Like many species of Filthy Lucre, you can't take it with you.

**14. d4?!          ed3**
**15. Qxd3          Qc7**

They're both in the middle of the ring, but soon only one guy is throwing punches.

Thus now White's *16. Nd2, 17. Ndf3* is right in principle, but a bit innocuous. Compare Black's 16th and 17th — *...0-0* and *...Rd8*. Ooof.

It still looks good to take a poke at the Knight — *16. b4 Nb7* — and then move two pieces (instead of *Nb1-f3*) — *17. Na3, 18. Bd2.*

Another possibility after *16. b4 Nb7* is *17. Qc4.* But I have my doubts, and I warn you away.... It *is* possible that a specific tactical continuation will work for an underdeveloped player, but that's rare. Don't even try. It's too much fun for Black. He could save his c-pawn with *17... c5* and have enough for his one pawn after *18. Qb5† Nd7* and *19... 0-0.*

But why sweat the c-pawn? White will waste more time than it's worth — *17. Qc4 Nd6 (17...*

*Be6!?) 18. Qxc6† Qxc6 19. Nxc6 Bb7 20. Nd4 0-0.* Analysis of this position is beyond me, but with ideas of *...Bxg2, ...Rfe8,* and *...Rac8* I'd rather play Black. White may live, but *I'd* be wishing I had kopied Kopylov. (You *knew* I couldn't resist that.) (Hey — I spared you "Luv to kopy Kopylov.")

| | | |
|---|---|---|
| **16.** | **Nd2** | **0-0** |
| **17.** | **Ndf3** | **Rd8** |
| **18.** | **Qc2** | **Be6** |

Last call for *19. b4!?*

| | | |
|---|---|---|
| **19.** | **Bd2?!** | **c5!** |

Fine move. Black sees that b2-b4 is worth preventing, even at the cost of temporarily restricting his Bishop on b6.

Now White should consider dropping the pawn halfway — *20. b3!?*, planning next or soon 0-0-0. I'm not entirely comfortable with this, but then it's an uncomfortable sort of position. The King seems safer on c1 than on e1 (two c-pawns, no e-pawns), and I'd like to use the

Queen's Rook. Black has enough for his pawn with ...Bd5-e4 or ...Nc6 (...Nb7!?) and ...a5-a4, but I think White has enough pieces in play to hold him off. Dynamic equality?

**20. c4?!**

It's hard to be too critical of this. He threatens *17. Bxa5 Bxa5† 18. Kf2*, the K/g1 finding a comparatively safe haven.

So he anticipates the game continuation. The problem is all too common when looking at specific "forcing" lines. You look at them with a bit of a bias, and the further you go along, the easier it seems to be to make things work out....

**20. ...            Nc6**
**21. Nxc6        Qxc6**

*Stop.* White should forget his analysis and think generally for a minute — *His King is safe, mine is on an open file in the center of the board. I'm a pawn up. What say I hide my King and develop my Queen's Rook — 0-0-0. There may be some grief associated with ...Ne4 (and ...Bf5?), but all my pieces will be developed in the center. If that's not adequate, there's no Justice.*

**22. Ne5**

Instead, he "gains time," seeing that Black can't take the g-pawn because of *23. Bf3* winning an exchange.

**22. ...            Qxg2!**

I suspect Bud found this the easiest move of the game.

**23. Bf3        Qxh2**
**24. Bxa8**

Otherwise, *he's* a pawn down, without enough for it (?) after *24. 0-0-0 Rac8 25. Rh1 Qf2.*

Now *24... Rxa8? 25. 0-0-0* is good for White.

**24. ...            Bf5!**

Who could resist? The white Queen must cover d2.

*24... Qh4†* may also be good, but the text adds the possibility of ...Ne4 to the mix.

Black uses his next move to stop 0-0-0 before he bags the Bishop on a8.

**25. Qc3        Qh4†**
**26. Ke2**

Looking for Rook activity and avoiding a pin on the d-file.

**26. ...            Rxa8**

**27. Rh1?**

Always always always look to development for an answer to your problems. Can Black win after *27. Rae1!?* Bud? Help! The best I see is *27... Bg4†* (to stop *Kd1-c1*) *28. Nxg4 Qxg4† 29. Qf3 Re8† 30. Kd1 Rxe1† 31. Bxe1 Qe6 △ ...Ne4* (and *...f5* if necessary), when I think it's probably a draw.

In the game, Black makes the same moves, but White has one effective Rook less. One Rook is a lot.

| 27. | ... | Bg4† |
| 28. | Nxg4 | Qxg4† |
| 29. | Qf3 | Re8† |
| 30. | Be3 | Qe6 |

With two threats — *...Qxc4†* and *...Ng4.* Can White defend both c4 and e3? ...

| 31. | Rac1 | Ng4 |
| 32. | Rc3 | Ba5! |

Not really. And *32... Nxe3 33. Rxe3 (33. Qxe3? Qd7) Qxc4†* could be played now, but it's important to have the Bishop on a5. It's the Theme of this Game — Black maximizes the activity of his pieces.

| 33. | Rd3 | Nxe3 |
| 34. | Rxe3 | Qxc4† |
| 35. | Kf2 | Qd4 |

Now, thanks to *32... Ba5!,* he threatens *36... Bd2.* Black is winning. *36. Ke2 Qd2†.*

| 36. | Rd1 | Rxe3 |
| 37. | Qxe3 | Qxd1 |
| 38. | Qe8† | Kh7 |
| 39. | Qxf7 | Be1† |
| 40. | Kg2 | Qe2† |

**41. Resigns.**

# ENVOI

Gentle Reader,

I hope the foregoing has been Stimulating and Rewarding and Challenging. Writing it was certainly all three.

But now, it's time to Relax. Let us part company enjoying the words of Lewis Carroll in his epic ...

## Gerzawocky

*'Twas brillig, and the slithy toves*
*Did gyre and gimble in the wabe;*
*All mimsy were the borogoves,*

*And the mome raths outgrabe.*

| | | |
|----|------|-----|
| 1. | e4 | g6 |
| 2. | d4 | Bg7 |
| 3. | Nc3 | c6 |
| 4. | Bc4 | d6 |
| 5. | Qf3 | e6 |
| 6. | Nge2 | b5 |
| 7. | Bb3 | Bb7 |
| 8. | 0-0 | Nd7 |
| 9. | Bf4 | Qe7 |
| 10. | Rad1 | e5 |
| 11. | Bg5 | |

*"Beware the Jabberwock, my son!*
*"The jaws that bite, the claws that catch!*
*"Beware the Jubjub bird, and shun*
*"The frumious Bandersnatch!"*

| | | |
|-----|-----|-----|
| 11. | ... | f6 |

| | | |
|-----|------|------|
| 12. | Bh4 | b4 |
| 13. | Na4 | Nh6 |
| 14. | Qd3 | Nf7 |
| 15. | Qc4 | a5 |

| | |
|-----|------|
| 16. | Qe6 |

16. Qxf7† Qxf7 17. Bxf7† Kxf7 18. de5 Nxe5 19. Rxd6 Ba6 20. Re1 Rad8 21. Rxd8 Rxd8 ...

White wins a pawn with this long line,
*But would it also win the Day?*
Rook swooping down looks Might Fine,
*So Black has Counterplay.*

| 16. | ... | Rd8 |
|-----|-----|-----|
| 17. | Qxe7† | Kxe7 |
| 18. | de5 | de5 |
| 19. | c3 | Nd6 |
| 20. | Bc2 | Bh6 |

He took his vorpal sword in hand:
*Long time the manxome foe he sought —*
So rested he by the Tumtum tree,
*And stook awhile in thought.*

| 21. | cb4 | ab4 |
|-----|-----|-----|
| 22. | b3 | c5 |
| 23. | f3 | Be3† |
| 24. | Bf2 | Bd4 |

It looked a draw with Bishop takes;
*Black then would push the Pawn c4.*
But d4-square an Outpost makes,
*And Black now wanted more.*

| 25. | Nxd4 | ed4 |
|-----|------|-----|
| 26. | e5 | fe5 |
| 27. | Bh4† | |

And as in uffish thought he stood,
*The Jabberwock, with eyes of flame,*
Came whiffling through the tulgey wood,
*And burbled as it came!*

| 27. | ... | Ke6 |
|-----|-----|-----|
| 28. | Bxd8 | Rxd8 |

| 29. | Nb2 | Nf5 |
|-----|-----|-----|
| 30. | Nc4 | Bd5 |
| 31. | Bd3 | |

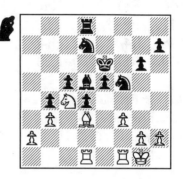

| 31. | ... | Bxc4 |
|-----|-----|------|
| 32. | Bxc4† | Kd6 |
| 33. | Rfe1 | Nb6 |
| 34. | Bd3 | Nd5 |
| 35. | Rd2 | Nfe3 |

About here it's not so very clear
*Just Who is doing What to Whom.*
Black's Knights, 'tis sure, are full of cheer
*But Rooks need much more room.*

| 36. | Be4 | Rd7 |
|-----|-----|-----|
| 37. | g3 | g5 |
| 38. | h3 | Ra7 |
| 39. | Bxd5 | Nxd5 |
| 40. | Rde2 | Ne3 |
| 41. | Kf2 | Ra3 |
| 42. | Kg1 | c4 |

One, two! One, two! And through and
through
*The vorpal blade went snicker-snack!*
He left it dead, and with its head
*He went galumphing back.*

| 43. | Rxe3 | de3 |
|-----|------|-----|
| 44. | Rxe3 | Rxa2 |
| 45. | bc4 | Kc5 |
| 46. | Rxe5† | Kxc4 |
| 47. | Re4† | Kb3 |
| 48. | h4 | gh4 |
| 49. | Rxh4 | Kc3 |

*"And hast thou slain the Jabberwock?*
*"Come to my arms, my beamish boy!*
*"O frabjous day! Callooh! Callay!"*
*He chortled in his joy.*

| 50. | Rxh7 | b3 |
|-----|------|-----|
| 51. | Rb7 | b2 |
| 52. | f4 | Kd4 |

Leo Whiteside 0–1 Stephan
Gerzadowicz
1991-93

*'Twas brillig, and the slithy toves*
*Did gyre and gimble in the wabe;*
*All mimsy were the borogoves,*
*And the mome raths outgrabe.*

# Colophon

This book was produced in Adobe's *Goudy Oldstyle* 12/14 in conjunction with Thinkers' Press' *C.R. Horowitz* chess font. World processing done in MS-Word 5.1® and Aldus' PageMaker 5.0a® on a Macintosh Centris 650. Initial Caps from Aridi.

Cover Design: Bob Long
Photography of Thinkers: Dick Oberg
Typographic Design: Bob Long
Copyediting: Bob Long
Proofers: Bob Long and Stephan Gerzadowicz